# The
# Recorder Player's
# Handbook

Hans-Martin Linde

# The Recorder Player's Handbook

**Translated from the German
by Richard Deveson**

ED 12322

London Mainz New York Paris Tokyo

First published in German under the title
Handbuch des Blockflötenspiels
First edition © B. Schott's Söhne, Mainz, 1962
Second edition (revised and enlarged) © B. Schott's Söhne, Mainz, 1984
English translation of the second edition
© 1991 Schott & Co. Ltd, London
British Library Cataloguing in Publication Data

Linde, Hans-Martin
    The recorder player's handbook. – 2nd ed
    I. Title    II. [Handbuch des Blockflötenspiels. *English*]
    788.36

ISBN 0 946535 17 5

ED 12322

Designed by Geoffrey Wadsley

Printed in England

# Contents

# Abbreviations

| | |
|---|---|
| AMW | Archiv für Musikwissenschaft |
| DDT | Denkmäler deutscher Tonkunst |
| DTÖ | Denkmäler der Tonkunst in Österreich |
| GA | Gesamtausgabe |
| MGG | Die Musik in Geschichte und Gegenwart |
| Amadeus | Amadeus Verlag, Zurich (available in UK from Schott, London) |
| Arch | Archive of Recorder Consorts, Schott, London |
| BA | Bärenreiter Ausgabe, Bärenreiter Verlag, Kassel |
| Bä HM | Hortus Musicus, Bärenreiter Verlag, Kassel |
| B & H | Breitkopf & Härtel, Wiesbaden |
| Boosey | Boosey & Hawkes, London |
| Dob | Doblinger, Vienna |
| Hä | Hännsler Verlag, Neuhausen-Stuttgart |
| Haslinger | Haslinger, Vienna |
| Hof | Friedrich Hofmeister, Hofheim |
| LPM | London Pro Musica Edition, Brighton |
| Moe | Moeck Verlag, Celle |
| Moes | Moeseler Verlag, Wolfenbüttel |
| MuRa | Musica Rara, Montreux |
| NMA | Nagels Musik Archiv, Bärenreiter Verlag, Kassel |
| Noe | Otto Heinrich Noetzel and Heinrichshofen's Verlag, Wilhelmshaven |
| OUP | Oxford University Press, Oxford |
| Pelikan | Musikverlag zum Pelikan, Zurich (now Hug & Co., Zurich) |
| Pe | C. F. Peters, Frankfurt am Main |
| Ri | G. Ricordi, Milan/Munich |
| S | B. Schott's Söhne, Mainz |
| SL | Schott & Co. Ltd, London |
| Siko | Musikverlag Hans Sikorski, Hamburg |
| Sirius | Sirius Verlag, Berlin (now Heinrichshofen/Noe) |
| SRP | Society of Recorder Players, Schott, London |

| UE | Universal Edition, Vienna/London |
| XYZ | XYZ, Amsterdam |
| Zen-On | Zen-On, Tokyo |
| ZfH | Zeitschrift für Hausmusik, Kassel |
| ZfS | Zeitschrift für Spielmusik, Celle (Moeck Verlag) |
| Zi | Wilhelm Zimmerman, Frankfurt am Main |

# Preface

This book originated in a course in recorder method given at the Schola Cantorum Basiliensis at the beginning of the 1960s. The basic outline of the book was drawn up at the suggestion of Schott, Mainz, and the first edition was published in 1962. Since then, recorder playing has made dramatic strides. There are now outstanding recorder players in all parts of the world who can stand comparison with virtuosos of other instruments. The recorder still has a special role in music teaching, but it has also made its way into the concert hall, and recordings involving the instrument are almost too many to number. There is world-wide interest in historical performance practice, yet at the same time modern works constitute a substantial part of the recorder literature now being performed.

It had therefore become a matter of some urgency to revise the *Handbook* in order to meet this new situation. The present edition retains the format of the old one, but account has been taken of new knowledge and methods with regard to historical and contemporary performance practice. The result has been some expansion as well as occasional re-ordering of the material. It was necessary at the time of original publication to give details of the very small number of recordings then available, but this has now become unnecessary. The bibliography has been revised in the light of current needs: a good number of items have been removed, while publications that have appeared in the interim have been added.

*Hans-Martin Linde*

*Translator's note*

For this second edition of *The Recorder Player's Handbook*, the German text has been entirely re-translated. I am most grateful to Edgar Hunt, Keith Hodgkinson and Clare Deveson for their generous help and advice.

*Richard Deveson*

# The Recorder

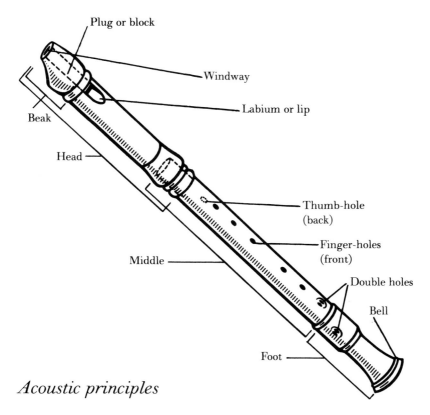

Plug or block

Windway

Labium or lip

Beak

Head

Thumb-hole
(back)

Finger-holes
(front)

Middle

Double holes

Bell

Foot

## *Acoustic principles*

The recorder is a tube, open at one end and closed off at the other by the device through which the air is blown. The principal distinguishing feature of all members of the flute family is an edge (or labium) that divides the air-stream. In the recorder, the height and width of the air-stream directed on to the labium are determined by the shape of a windway. The method of sound production thus differs from that used in the transverse flute, where the air-stream is shaped by the player's lips. As the air-stream from the narrow windway of the recorder meets the labium, alternating eddies of air are created on the upper and lower sides of the labium edge. Some of this eddying air enters the bore of the recorder along the under side of the labium, while the rest passes outwards above the labium edge. The eddies on the under side rotate clockwise, and those on the upper side anticlockwise, the former eddies causing an air-stream to vibrate. This sound is called an 'edge-tone'. The contact of the eddies of air with the labium edge creates a compression wave, the reflection of which reacts with the formation of the next eddy from the windway. The vibrating air-stream is capable of setting up resonance vibrations in the column of air within the body of the recorder.

The air molecules within the recorder vibrate along the axis of the tube (constituting longitudinal waves). Their motion is determined by alternations in pressure produced by the edge-tone. The rate of movement of these air molecules (their frequency of vibration) influences the pitch of the sound: the greater the frequency, the higher the pitch, and the lower the frequency, the lower the pitch. The vibrating air-column produces so-called standing waves. The stationary points on such waves are called wave nodes, while the points of highest amplitude are called wave antinodes. The smaller the distance between the nodes, the more rapid is the frequency and, correspondingly, the higher the pitch.

The simplest mode of vibration (fundamental vibration) produces the fundamental note of the recorder. This is the instrument's lowest harmonic, produced when all the finger-holes are closed; it has the greatest wave-length for the length of the tube in question. The velocity of the air molecules is at its highest (a velocity antinode) at the open end of the tube, whereas the pressure is at its lowest (a pressure node). Combined with this fundamental frequency

Sequence of movement of eddies at the recorder labium

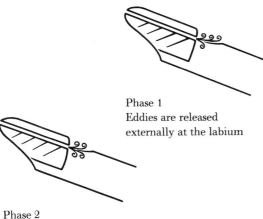

Phase 1
Eddies are released
externally at the labium

Phase 2
Air-stream is deflected
downwards

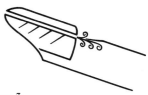

Phase 3
Eddies pass into the bore of
the instrument

are a certain number of shorter frequencies. The partials or harmonics thus produced are called overtones. They are responsible for the distinctive timbre of the recorder sound. Sounds higher than the fundamental are produced by opening the finger-holes. Each time a hole is opened, the vibrating air-column is shortened: the end of the recorder tube is, in effect, shifted.

Pitch can also be altered by changing the breath-pressure. In the words of Martin Agricola:[1]

*Die untersten acht Töne ganz messig blas*
*Die andern sieben etwas schneller las*
*Die nechstē vier begerē ein schnellern wind*
*Die öbirsten ij gehē ganz geschwind*

(Blow the lowest eight notes quite gently; the next seven a little more quickly. The next four need a quicker breath, and the top notes go very fast)

Breath-pressure on the recorder, at between 10 and 40 mm of water (roughly .001 to .004 atmospheres), is significantly lower than with most other wind instruments. A test of the purity of an instrument is the extent to which it gives an even relationship between breath-pressure and loudness, while preserving purity of intonation. The modern demand for good intonation over a chromatic scale of at least two octaves poses a considerable challenge to recorder makers. Indeed, this is the reason why many of the cheap recorders now on the market are inferior in quality.

The level of breath-pressure, and thus the speed of the breath flow, affect the acoustic make-up of the sound. As breath-pressure increases, an increase in the edge-tone frequency and in the pitch of the fundamental can be heard. If the breath-pressure is stepped up further, the edge-tone frequency gradually approaches that of the second harmonic of the instrument. Beyond a certain degree of pressure this pitch becomes stronger than the fundamental. If this happens unintentionally, the player speaks of a 'break' or 'squeak' in the note. When done in controlled fashion, the process is known as overblowing. Except, however, in the case of certain woodwind instruments (transverse flutes and the baroque oboe) and of organ pipes, overblowing is normally effected by the use of an octave key or an overblowing hole. With the recorder, it is done by opening the thumb-hole by about one tenth. This doubles the frequency of the note being fingered, so producing the octave. The wider the bore of the instrument, the harder it is to get the overblown notes to 'speak'. So-called 'Renaissance flutes' are a case in point: these earlier instruments are wider-bored than recorders of the later baroque type and their compass is therefore necessarily smaller (on the treble from f′ to d‴) than that of the baroque instrument, which spans a good two and a half octaves.

The ratio of the length of a tube to its width, known in organ building as scaling, is of vital importance. Generally speaking, in tubes with wide scaling only the lowest harmonics are produced at significant amplitudes. Wide-bore recorders therefore have a sound dominated by the fundamental, often a rather dull one. The smaller the width in relation to the length, the greater the number of higher overtones in the acoustic make-up of the sound. Narrow scaling in recorders thus makes for a weak low register, wide scaling for a strong one. The strongly fundamental-dominated sound of wide-bore instruments is particularly noticeable when they are made of wood; it is much less apparent in metal instruments. Sounds which are low in overtones do not blend well with other instruments, so that if one melodic line is meant to stand out very clearly from another, then an instrument with a stronger fundamental is particularly suitable.

The pitch of a note also depends on the rate at which the successive eddies of air strike the edge of the labium, the interval between the eddies being governed by the distance between the windway and the labium. If the distance from the windway to the labium edge is small, the pitch of the note is higher than if the distance is large.

A very narrow labium produces a relatively quiet sound with few overtones. The greater the width of the labium, the greater the strength of all the partials: increasing the size of the labium is tantamount to increasing the energy that activates the recorder's sound. If the sides of the windway are high, a bright, attractive sound results, whereas low sides give a more open, mellow timbre. The roof of the windway can be curved to a greater or lesser degree, or it can be flat.

Temperature can have a significant effect on pitch. If the temperature of a vibrating air-column is altered, the velocity of sound, and hence the frequency, is also altered. By nature, thin-walled instruments are particularly sensitive even to quite small alterations in temperature. Recorder players know from experience that the pitch of the instrument rises as the instrument becomes warmer and falls as the temperature decreases.

The nature and strength of the material of which the instrument is made also affect the sound. Recorders made of firm, dense wood have a more powerful sound than those made of soft wood. Instruments made of harder wood also have a greater range of tone colour: the higher harmonics can be obtained more easily and have a more attractive sound.

The size and positioning of the finger-holes plays a vital part in the vibration processes within the tube of the recorder. This is why the finger-holes are unequally spaced and why they are bored at differing angles. Broadly speaking, the upper rims of the finger-holes affect the notes of the lower octave, and the lower rims the upper octave. Thus if d′′′ is too flat, the maker enlarges the lower rim of the next open finger-hole, while if d′′ is too sharp the upper rim of the hole is made smaller with shellac or a similar material. Pitch is also affected by the degree of bevelling on the finger-holes as they go into the instrument.

Additional differences arise from the shape of the bore. The acoustic properties of a resonating tube can be precisely predicted only if the bore is cylindrical. Since the recorder, however, has an inverted conical bore, the maker has to rely on trial and error and past experience. The distinctive characteristic of conical flutes is their sweet, warm sound: the baroque *traverso*, as well as the recorder, has this kind of bore. The cylindrical Böhm flute is notable for its more powerful fundamental, but the cylindrical bore also means that 'the sound spectrum becomes more disharmonic'.[2]

A final factor affecting recorder sound is breath-pressure. Certain recorders, because of the way in which they are constructed (e.g. the narrowness of the windway), permit only a comparatively small amount of breath pressure. Overtones, however, can be brought out only if sound production is reasonably forceful. Recorders of this kind therefore have a timbre particularly low in overtones.

## Materials

Wood has always been the preferred material for making recorders. Francis Bacon described the influence of the material on the sound as follows:[3] 'When the sound is created between the blast of the mouth and the air of the pipe, it hath nevertheless some communication with the matter of the sides of the pipe, and the spirits in them contained.'

A study of the catalogues of a number of instrument collections[4] shows the following range of materials used in recorder making:

| | | | |
|---|---|---|---|
| boxwood | 38 | palisander | 2 |
| ivory | 27 | jacaranda | 1 |
| maple | 7 | apple | 1 |
| ebony | 6 | poplar | 1 |
| pear | 5 | nutwood | 1 |
| plum | 5 | glass | 1 |
| cherry | 3 | marble | 1 |
| beech | 3 | tortoiseshell | 1 |

There are 73 wooden instruments on this list, as against 30 made from other materials. We should bear in mind that the strikingly large number of ivory instruments is due not only to their undisputed sound qualities but to the fact that the material was then of great value. Marin Mersenne,[5] writing about materials used in recorder making, says:

> They may be made of plum, cherry or other kinds of wood that can easily be bored; but generally wood of a pleasant colour is used, which may be given a beautiful finish, so that the quality of the instrument is equalled by its beauty, and the eye can, as it were, partake of the pleasure of the ear. Usually they are made of boxwood [...]

Boxwood recorders, indeed, are easily the largest category in instrument collections. Boxwood is particularly suitable for recorders by virtue of its hardness and density. But other hardwoods such as ebony, granadilla, palisander, cocobolo, olive, jacaranda and rosewood are equally suitable and in some respects give a finer sound than boxwood. Such precious woods were used less commonly in the past because of the high cost of imported timber.

Recorders made from pear, plum, walnut and maple wood have a rather gentler tone. These woods are less dense, and the inner wall of the instrument is liable to be rough. Recorders made from these woods are therefore often treated with cellulose or impregnated with paraffin. Although some of these instruments undoubtedly give a good sound and 'speak' well – and in the final analysis the art of the recorder maker is what counts here – those made of precious woods have a much more characteristic timbre.

The most suitable wood for recorder making is free of knots and has a close grain that is as straight as possible. This helps ensure that the inner surface remains smooth after drilling. Recorders with highly fibrous inner walls are less likely to produce a high-quality sound. As far as the durability of the various woods is concerned, it should be noted that although the harder woods are less easy to play in, they retain their optimum tone quality for a longer period. Softer woods are generally much easier to play in, but although a soft-wood instrument often gives a delightful sound at first, the bloom is rather quickly lost and the instrument will be played out more quickly.

Even in the past ivory recorders were great rarities. They were often fitted out with gold or silver keys and stored in magnificent cases. The inventory of instruments at the court of the Prince of Baden in 1582[6] refers to '[...] Four ivory flutes with gilt cases/ A case with ten boxwood flutes [...]' Ivory instruments have a clear, strong sound, and it is easier to produce dynamic differences on them without fluctuations of pitch than it is on wooden instruments. On the other hand, wood has a warmer timbre than the somewhat cool sound of ivory. Like wood, ivory is affected by changes in temperature and humidity. According to J. J. Ribock,[7] ivory is notable for 'swelling too easily', though also for its 'elegance of tone'. The weight of an ivory recorder is considerably greater than that of a wooden one: even a tenor recorder is difficult to hold, and a bass can be played only if the instrument is supported on a stand. Many ivory recorders go sharp after a few months, and if you are buying one you should make sure that the instrument is, if anything, initially under-pitched rather than over-pitched.

In recent years instruments have also been mass-produced in plastic. These instruments are robust and relatively unaffected by changes in temperature. If manufactured carefully, they even 'speak' more easily than many wooden recorders. There are now very many recorders made of synthetic materials on the market, some of them produced to baroque specifications. Nevertheless, as matters stand at present, the tone quality of recorders made from natural materials is generally to be preferred.

## Names for recorders

| | |
|---|---|
| *Common flute* | Term used in England in seventeenth and eighteenth centuries for treble recorder in f' |
| *Czakan* | Common in Hungary and Slav countries; still played today. Six finger-holes in front; no thumb-hole. Over-blown by increasing the supply of air |
| *Dolzflöte* | Transverse recorder (illustration in Praetorius, *Theatrum Instrumentorum*, Plate IX) |
| *Doppelflöte* | Two basic types: <br> a) With non-matching finger-holes: each of the two instruments therefore has its own system of fingering <br> b) *Akkordflöte* or chordal flute (eighteenth century, Chr. Schlegel, Basle): matching finger-holes, with each finger covering two holes at a time |
| *Douçaine (douchaine)* | Medieval French term for recorder. In the Middle Ages a distinction was made between *fleustes* (transverse flutes) and *douchaines* (recorders) |
| *Fiauto* | In Italy and Germany (Praetorius), seventeenth and eighteenth centuries, term denoting recorder |
| *Fipple flute* | Term sometimes used in England in more recent period instead of 'recorder' |
| *Flageolet(t)* | a) French (true) flageolet with two thumb-holes and four front finger-holes, fitted with sponge-chamber after *c*.1750 <br> b) English flageolet with only one thumb-hole. |

|  | The twin thumb-holes are the principal difference between the true flageolet and the normal recorder. The *flauto piccolo* often called for in eighteenth-century music (e.g. by Handel) is frequently a flageolet |
|---|---|
| *Flautino* | High recorder (piccolo or sopranino in f″), but also flageolet |
| *Flauto* | In Germany and Italy, almost always denotes the recorder (up to and including first decades of eighteenth century) |
| *Flauto di voce* and *voice flute* | Term used in England for recorder in d′. |

Compass:

| *Flauto piccolo* | In Praetorius, '*Klein Flöitlein*': piccolo/sopranino recorder, generally in f″. Used in Handel's operas (*Rinaldo, Richard I, Acis and Galatea, Alcina*), the *Water Music* and Bach's Cantatas BWV 96 and 103 (range in the first of these corresponds to that of the flageolet, as often in Handel) |
|---|---|
| *Flute* | In England, synonym for 'recorder' until eighteenth century. Later used to denote transverse flute, replacing the term 'German flute' |
| *Flûte à bec* | Term commonly used in France and Germany to denote treble recorder |
| *Flûte douce* | Synonym for *flûte à bec*; the term refers to the instrument's 'pleasant quietness'[8] |
| *Flûte pastourelle* | Also *flûte du quatre*; in England, 'fourth-flute'. |

Compass:

| *Recorder* | English term for all members of the recorder family |
|---|---|
| *Sixth-flute* | Variant of the common flute, first half of the eighteenth century, pitched a sixth higher (d″). Concertos for the sixth-flute by Baston, Babell, etc. |

Compass:

| *Schnabelflöte* | German term used only in eighteenth century; translation of *flûte à bec* (beaked flute) |

| | |
|---|---|
| *Schwegel* | Old High German, *suegula*. Originally, a term denoting all pipes. From *c*.1000 onwards, cylindrical one-hand recorder with two finger-holes and a thumb-hole. In France, *galoubet*. Usually played with side drum. Still in use in the seventeenth century, chiefly in dance and military music |

## Design

If we study the large number of pictorial representations of recorders, the descriptions of instruments found in contemporary treatises, and the fairly small number of actual instruments that survive, we can see that significant changes in the physical appearance of the recorder have taken place. These changes came about, as one would expect, as a result of the constant growth in the tonal and musical demands which the instrument had to meet in the course of its history.

No instruments of the medieval period survive. The earliest pictorial representations come from eleventh-century France and twelfth-century England.[9] Galpin notes[10] that illustrations in a Glasgow University Psalter (twelfth century) and in a volume in the Bodleian Library (thirteenth century) very probably represent recorders. Although early illustrations are difficult to interpret, it is apparent that the flutes shown in them differ only in minor ways from the windway or fipple flutes used in south- and west-European folk music. The distinguishing feature of these instruments is a smooth, continuous bore, usually cylindrical though occasionally slightly conical. As yet there is no bell on the foot joint. We do not know for certain how many finger-holes were present, but it is likely that there were already seven by the thirteenth century.

The bell developed in the course of the fifteenth century. Since the inverted conical bore had meanwhile been introduced, there can have been no acoustic reason for this innovation: clearly, there was a desire to add ornamentation to the smooth outline of the instrument. The recorders illustrated by Sebastian Virdung[11] are still quite smooth, but have small bells; the cylindrical bore seems by now to be the exception. The important features are the wide scaling, the narrow labium and the large distance between edge and windway. The tone of these instruments is full and mellow; their range is about one and a half octaves.

The first division of the tube occurred at the foot. The main reason for this was probably that if a revolving foot joint was used, only one hole for the little finger was needed. Previously a double hole for the little finger had been

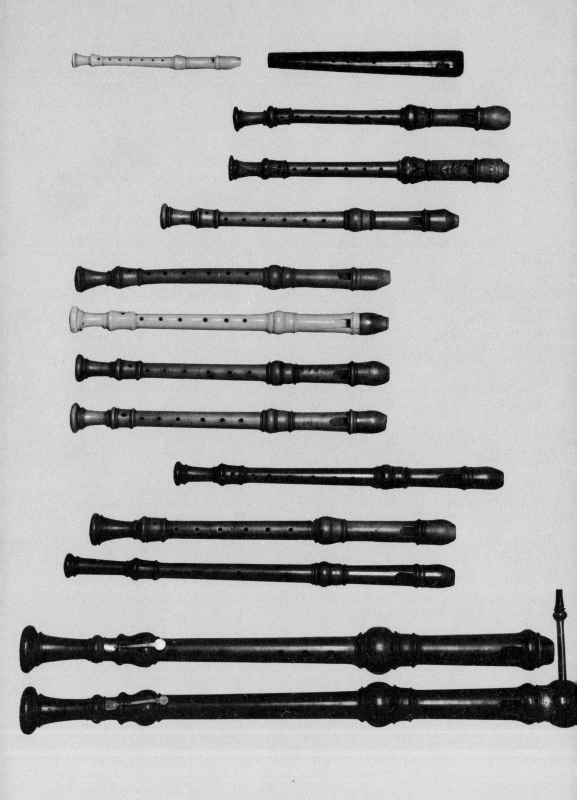

customary because it allowed two different ways of holding the instrument. Depending on whether the right or left hand was held uppermost, one or other of the double holes was plugged with wax.

By the seventeenth century at the latest the head and middle joints were also separated. Michael Praetorius describes the resulting gains in intonation:[12] 'The notion then came to me, to divide the upper part of the flute, midway between the mouth-hole and the finger-holes, and to make the upper part longer by two fingers' width. This part might then be inserted into the lower part as far as was necessary or desired, thus making the pipe longer or shorter [...]' The protuberances at the points where the head and middle joints and middle and foot joints meet were added in order to ensure that the instrument remained sturdy now that its walls had become thinner. In due course these protuberances were embellished with ivory or by carving.

It had become necessary at an early stage, especially with the larger recorders, to add one or more keys for those finger-holes that were difficult to reach. A bass instrument with two keys, for example, is known to have been built by the Bassani brothers of London in the sixteenth century.[13] Key mechanisms were housed in a variety of wooden or metal protective caps or fontanelles.

The beak of the recorder was usually rounded on the front and flattened off on the back, so that the mouthpiece could rest more easily on the lower lip. Large recorders were often played by means of an S-shaped crook leading into the top of the instrument, from which the windway directed the air-stream on to the labium edge. In other cases the air was blown directly, i.e. without the use of a crook. Direct contact via a beak makes for more precise articulation than is possible with a crook.

Recorder building today naturally relies heavily on historical precedent. At the same time, however, the recorder maker must decide what range of uses he envisages for the instrument. On the one hand, he can build an instrument which is as faithful as possible to a historical model but which will therefore be confined to a clearly restricted type of music. On the other hand, he can build a

Facing page (top to bottom): Sopranino recorder in f'', ivory (Johann Chr. Denner, early 18th century); double recorder (Christian Schlegel, first half of the 18th century); treble recorder in f' (F. Lehner, 18th century); treble recorder in f', ivory (18th century); treble recorder in f' (Joh. Chr. Denner); treble recorder in f' (H. Schell, first half of the 18th century); treble recorder in e' flat (18th century); tenor recorder in d' (Rippert, early 18th century); treble recorder in g' (18th century); treble recorder in g' (17th century); treble recorder in f' (Christian Schlegel); tenor recorder in d' (18th century); bass recorder in g (Christian Schlegel); bass recorder in f (Christian Schlegel)

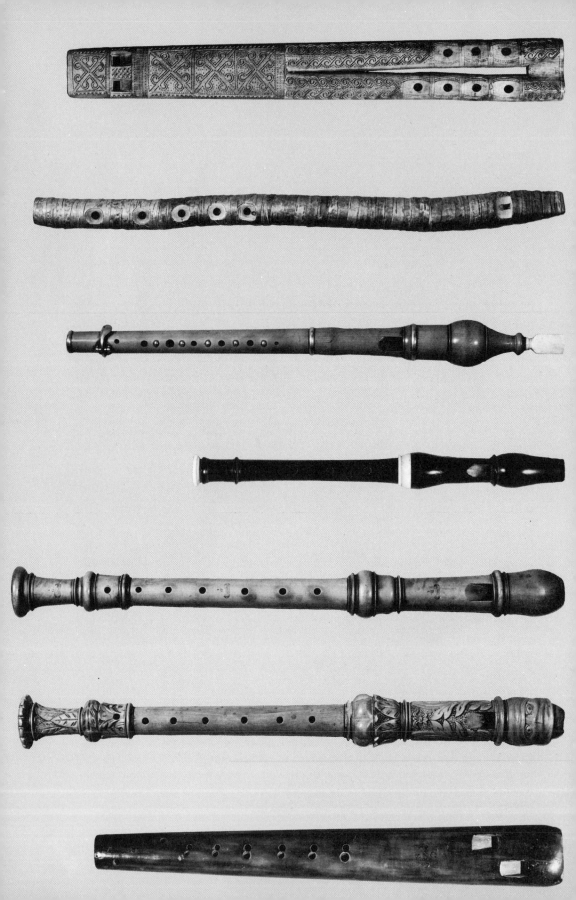

less specialized instrument suitable not only for early music but also for more general use. A great variety of instruments is now available, of all sorts of periods and styles. The main types are the medieval instrument, the Renaissance recorder, the baroque recorder, and a more neutral instrument which can perhaps be termed a 'modern' type. This wealth of choice is a good thing, and we should beware of seeing all virtue in one type alone. It is undeniable, however, that interest in historical recorder models, in particular, has grown to an enormous extent in recent years.

This is especially true of baroque recorders, which can be built to all sorts of historical models. The windway is almost always relatively narrow and slightly curved in these instruments, with the curvature usually concave lengthways and convex breadthways. This method of construction makes for a better concentration of air directed on to the labium, with the result (though not in all cases) that dynamic range is increased with only minimal alteration of pitch. On a recorder of this kind, therefore, a crescendo and diminuendo on a single note can usually be played without any perceptible distortion of intonation. It should also be noted, however, that even these baroque models are not entirely insensitive to changes in breath-pressure. The final authority must always be the player's ear. In the words of Bartolomeo Bismantova:[14] 'Care must also be taken that breath is applied to the instrument in such a way that there is neither increase nor decrease of pitch.'

The finger-holes of the baroque recorder are drilled conically, becoming wider towards the inside. The angle of drilling is by no means necessarily the same at all points on the finger-holes. The result is a fuller sound with richer colouring. Double holes for holes 6 and 7 are fairly uncommon on original instruments (see p. 10). The notes f' and g' are stronger without double holes, while the notes f' sharp and g' sharp are used rather rarely in baroque recorder music. In the absence of double holes these latter notes are obtained by half-opening the hole; otherwise the melodic line must be adjusted. (See, for example, modifications of voice-leading in the recorder parts in Bach's cantatas.)

Baroque instruments tend to be built to unequal temperament: original fingering tables are extremely instructive in this respect. It should never be forgotten, however, that in the last analysis intonation is governed by the way in which the performer actually plays the instrument.

Facing page (top to bottom): Yugoslav double recorder; Finnish shepherd's flute (Teppo Repo, Helsinki); English flageolet (A. Rieger, Munich, c.1800); French flageolet (J. P. Weih, 18th century); treble recorder in f' (Johann Christoph Denner, Nuremberg, early 18th century); treble recorder in g' (17th century); double recorder (Christian Schlegel, Basle, first half of the 18th century)

Pitch was variable in the period around 1700. It is not correct to say that the frequency a$'$ = 415 (i.e. a semitone below a$'$ = 440) was the '*alte Kammerton*' pure and simple. Pitch at that time varied between roughly a whole tone and a semitone lower than modern standard pitch, and was particularly low in France. Instruments of the flute family gain from lower pitch, their sound taking on more of the 'pleasant quietness' mentioned by Walther. The effect is particularly noticeable in the high register of the recorder and in the higher members of the flute family.

## Choosing an instrument

Only a good recorder player can judge whether a particular instrument is suitable for the purposes for which it is required. It is therefore best to take advice from an expert if you are not sure that you can assess the quality of a recorder yourself. Unfortunately, it is still generally the case that people will buy a recorder without consulting an expert in the way that they would naturally do when choosing a violin or an orchestral transverse flute. This is undoubtedly one of the reasons why so many mediocre instruments are available and why the standard of recorder playing is often so low. Only a few recorder dealers are themselves players and thus able to evaluate the quality of the instruments they have on sale. Going solely by a price list, even with instruments made by a firm with a good reputation, provides no guarantee that the instrument you choose will be a bargain or that it will prove satisfactory in the long run. As with any purchase, it is worth remembering that cheapest is rarely best. A recorder maker will devote more care to the manufacture of an expensive special instrument than he can to cheap mass-produced ones. It is certainly true that many manufacturers produce good instruments at reasonable prices, but a fine sound, pure intonation, flawless workmanship at a high degree of durability are possible only if an instrument has been made from first-rate materials and if sufficient time has been devoted to it.

The characteristics of different types of woods have already been described above (see p. 6). Here we shall discuss a number of other factors to be borne in mind when choosing an instrument. (All pitch references are to the treble recorder.)

### a) External condition

The external appearance of the recorder must inspire confidence. Wood without knots and with a close parallel grain is preferable. Beware of hidden defects such as incipient cracks, which can sometimes look like scratches on the outer surface of the wood. The joints should be particularly carefully inspected for signs of cracking. The labium and the finger-holes should be cleanly finished, and the inside surface of the instrument should be smooth and free of fibres. The plug must fit firmly enough not to change position under light finger pressure. The windway should be free of fibres and small impurities. The joints should fit well: it is better to have an instrument which sits together solidly than one whose component parts are loose. It is hard to gauge sound quality if an instrument is not airtight, although it may be a straightforward matter to make adjustments (e.g. by having the cork lappings replaced or thickened).

### b) Sound quality

To test the tone of the instrument, play the notes $c''$ and $c'''$, which should sound clear and free of background noise. Check the octaves $f'-f''-f'''$, too, for their tonal range. The dynamic range of the instrument should also be established. Some recorders vary relatively little in intonation whether blown loudly or quietly, while others perceptibly rise or fall in pitch in response to the smallest change in breath-pressure. Instruments of the first sort are usually preferable. A recorder with a thin or excessively delicate sound is not suitable unless required for a quite special purpose. In general, it should be remembered that when played in the home and, *a fortiori*, in public, the recorder has to hold its own against other instruments. Naturally, it is also important whether the instrument is going to be used with other early instruments or in a modern ensemble. The finer nuances of timbre (open, bright, nasal, dark or mellow colouring) must ultimately be matters of personal taste.

### c) Intonation

You should deliberately choose an instrument which is just below pitch when cold or which, when warm, can be tuned to pitch if extended very slightly.

Check specifically that the octaves $f'-f''$, $g'-g''$, $a'-a''$ and $d''-d'''$ are in tune. On some models of instruments, $g'$ and $a'$ tend to be too sharp and $d''$ too flat or $d'''$ too sharp. Any fault of intonation, however, is logically possible. Whatever flaws are present within the basic scale of F should be so small that they can be compensated for without difficulty. As far as semitone fingerings are concerned, $c'''$ sharp tends to sound flat in terms of modern equal temperament, and you should make sure that it is possible to raise the pitch by a slight increase in breath-pressure, should this be necessary. The note $f''$ sharp, which can be played with several different fingerings, should also be carefully checked: it should be possible to play it acceptably in tune at least with the principal fingering (1 and 2) and with the thumb alone (see p. 36). When checking b′ and c″ sharp, do not forget that often these notes will sound true only if the two lowest fingers of the right hand half-close the double holes.

*d) 'Speech'*

A good recorder should respond or 'speak' well in all registers, though special attention should be paid to the lowest and highest registers. A ready response in staccato as well as legato (rapid note-repetitions and rapid scales or broken chords with and without modern double-tonguing) is an important index of an instrument's quality. The transition b″–c‴ sharp should 'speak' easily both slurred and tongued. Leaps such as f′–f″ and f″–f‴ should also be checked.

Finally, the following general considerations may be useful to anyone buying a new recorder:

1. Try to listen objectively and to establish the distinctive characteristics of the instrument. It is easy to make the mistake of judging a new instrument in the light of an old and familiar one.
2. There is no such thing as a recorder with absolutely correct intonation, any more than there are 'perfect' oboes or transverse flutes. A recorder blown with equal breath-pressure throughout its two octaves will not be perfectly in tune. Shortcomings in intonation must be overcome by breathing technique. Whether an instrument can be played in tune therefore depends on how large these 'built-in' discrepancies of pitch actually are.
3. Recorder makers cannot be expected to turn out identical instruments. You should certainly choose an instrument, however, whose maker can easily be contacted if alterations or repairs need to be made.

## Care of the instrument

The labium is the most delicate part of the recorder. Under no circumstances should its sharp edge be damaged, as the tone quality of the instrument will be considerably impaired. Care should also be taken that the upper surface of the labium (the notch) is kept free of dirt, fluff, water droplets etc.

The purpose of the windway is to direct the air as accurately as possible on to the labium, and it must therefore be kept free of dirt. When cleaning is necessary, a feather or strip of paper should be used, but do not push right through to the labium edge. If a lot of dirt has built up, the plug can be removed. If this is necessary, do not play the recorder for a few days beforehand, as it is easier to remove the plug when it is dry than when it is even slightly swollen; it should not be forced off. Any deposit on the surface of the plug can then be removed with very fine sandpaper. Under no circumstances should any of the wood itself be scraped off, as this alters the height of the windway. Special care must always be taken when replacing the plug. If the plug is especially swollen, the windway becomes narrowed, making the instrument's tone thinner and leading to frequent clogging. In this case, the plug should be replaced by the maker.

It is not unusual for a recorder to develop a certain roughness of tone, especially after a period of sustained use. How rough the tone becomes depends on temperature and humidity, as well as on the construction of the instrument and the player's technique. Recorders are often sensitive to weather conditions, especially to warmth and dampness. The breath temperature of the individual player can also be a significant factor affecting the build-up of condensation in the windway. Clogging can largely be avoided by 'silent' blowing or by rubbing or warming the head joint, particularly, between the hands or in one's pocket before playing. A recorder should be sufficiently warmed before use so as not to get appreciably warmer while actually being played. If necessary, moisture can be removed from the windway by blowing. The common practice, however, of clearing the instrument by blowing while covering the labium edge with the finger can be shown to have a harmful effect. Over a long period the strong current of air and the contact with the labium edge tend to wear away the edge. It is better to free the accumulated moisture from the windway by rapidly sucking upwards. In stubborn cases the head joint can be removed and closed at the lower end with the flat of the hand, and, by blowing into the labium, one can then remove the moisture upwards through the top of the windway.

The inner wall of the recorder tube has a great influence on timbre and strength of sound. It must be kept particularly free of fibres, fluff and dust. After playing, therefore, wipe the instrument out thoroughly. A mop for a transverse flute is suitable (i.e. a rod with an eyelet for the cloth) but a piece of silk or cotton is more absorbent than the usual sort of commercial recorder mop and does not leave fluff behind. It also gives a better polish to the inner wall. The moisture produced by playing will be distributed evenly only if the bore is polished smooth. A recorder produces its best sound, not when it is completely dry, but when the inner walls are covered with a light coating of moisture. Francis Bacon wrote:[15] 'A pipe a little moistened on the inside [...] maketh a more solemn sound, than if the pipe were dry. [...] The cause is, for that all things porous being superficially wet, [...] become a little more even and smooth, and if the body that createth the sound be clean and smooth, it maketh it sweeter.'

Recorders made of non-impregnated wood should be oiled every two or three months. If you are dissatisfied with your instrument and hand it in to a maker for overhaul, it is quite likely that he will do no more than polish and oil the bore. The oil required can be obtained in music shops. Other non-acidic oils can also be used: pure (not boiled) linseed oil, almond oil and banana oil are all reliable, though not olive oil. Oil should not be applied too cold, because if it is viscous it cannot penetrate the pores of the wood properly. The whole inner surface of the recorder should be oiled evenly using a wiper, so that its appearance is uniformly shiny. Under no circumstances let oil touch the plug or labium. After oiling, the instrument should not be touched for at least a day, to allow the oil to be absorbed into the wood. Set the recorder down with the finger-holes uppermost, because if any remaining drops of oil go hard they will reduce the size of the holes and alter the tuning.

When assembling the recorder, be careful not to fit the joints at a slant. Take hold of the joints by the ends and push them together with a gentle rotating movement. The lappings on the joints should be checked periodically, as even a small air leak can adversely affect the sound. Poor 'speech' in the lower notes may be caused by insufficiently tight lapping. Lappings can easily be renewed with thread, which should be strong but not too thick. Many recorders have joints lapped with cork. Cork which has shrunk will re-expand if held over a flame while being rotated continuously. If the recorder is difficult to assemble, the joints can be lubricated with cork grease, which can be bought in music shops. This will also go a long way to preventing the cork from crumbling. If the end of a joint regularly gets very swollen, the inside of the section of the instrument into which the joint is inserted can be gently smoothed with fine sandpaper. The action of the upper part of the thumb against the thumb-hole can sometimes damage the rim of the hole, and this can affect the 'speech' of the notes in the upper register. The thumbnail should therefore be kept cut short, and care should be taken not to apply the thumb too forcefully while playing. A recorder maker can repair a damaged thumb-hole by mounting a ring made of ivory or plastic.

A new instrument must be played in very gently. Play only for brief spells at first, say half an hour a day; after about a week the playing time can be gradually increased. The high notes should not be too severely tested at the outset. It is more important to concentrate on producing a rounded, resonant tone than to practise rapid and highly staccato virtuoso passage work. Many instruments have been ruined from the start by being played too fast, too coarsely or too clumsily. Occasionally changes in intonation will become apparent after a period of use. If so, you should ask the maker to check the instrument.

A recorder should never be kept directly next to a source of heat. Dry air caused by central heating is extremely harmful to wood, so ensure that the air is sufficiently humid. If you have an expensive recorder it is worth buying a hygrometer.

If an instrument is not used for a long period the diameter of the bore may contract. This will upset the entire tuning of the instrument. Even instruments that are played only rarely should therefore be oiled from time to time. Better still, of course, the instrument should be played regularly.

If possible, do not lend your instrument to another player. It is an odd but well-attested fact that the sound can 'go off'. Differences in the way the instrument is blown and cleaned, and in breath temperature and dampness, can often lead to perceptible changes in timbre and 'speech' after an instrument has been borrowed.

Finally, a recorder is best kept in a case rather than in a plastic holder. A solid case gives best protection against damage; plastic holders are often so airtight that the instrument cannot dry out properly.

# 2

## Playing the Recorder

*Breathing and sound production*

To produce musical sounds, the wind player must combine various positions and movements of the facial muscles, the lips, the teeth, the mouth and throat muscles, and the respiratory organs. Breath control is of paramount importance. The art of wind playing consists in allying voluntary, or controlled, breathing – the type of breathing required for the specific purpose of playing a wind instrument – to the musical meaning of the piece being played. In controlled breathing, exhalation lasts considerably longer than inhalation. The starting of the breath, its prolongation over time, its retention and ending are all features subject to control. Unlike the natural method of breathing through the nose, controlled breathing necessarily occurs through the mouth. The only time the player breathes through the nose is at the beginning of a piece or before resuming playing after a pause.

The breathing process

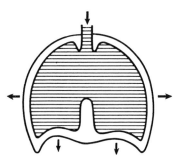

*Breathing in*
Rib cage expands,
diaphragm is lowered and
flattens, lungs fill with air

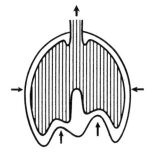

*Breathing out*
Rib cage contracts,
diaphragm arches upwards,
air leaves lungs

*a)  The breathing process*

The most important respiratory organ is the diaphragm, which separates the chest from the abdominal cavity, stretching right across the trunk. The diaphragm is irregular in shape, with two curved portions forming an arch slightly flattened in the middle which extends upwards into the rib cage. In contrast with the other respiratory organs (the muscles of the chest and stomach), its functioning depends on the flow of breath. Inhalation requires muscular action. As contraction takes place, the diaphragm gradually flattens, exerting downward pressure on the abdominal organs. This, together with the application of the elevator rib muscles and intercostal muscles, causes the chest cavity to expand; at the same time, the rib cage expands in all directions. In deep breathing the stomach muscles also expand somewhat with each inhalation. Ideally this latter muscular action does not lead to an obvious protusion of the stomach, though this often occurs in practice. If the rim of the rib cage expands properly in all directions, the other correct muscular actions will follow suit.

In wind playing, breathing in has to be done rapidly: prolonged inhalation is the exception. Particularly rapid supplementary breathing (snatched breathing) is necessary mainly in passages of fast continuous notes, when the inhalation time may often be less than half a second. In such circumstances, frequent snatched breathing may be necessary to ward off the unsteady sound caused by a lack of breath. Very long notes need to be started very gently and require an even flow of breath.

Breathing out is accompanied by the relaxation of the relevant respiratory muscles. The diaphragm relaxes again and gradually reverts to its original arched shape. It should exert a downward pressure in both inhalation and exhalation, to counteract the force of the lungs. This downward pressure is greater with inhalation than with exhalation, but its direction remains the same. The common assumption that the diaphragm expels the air upwards is a false one and has been disproved in a number of studies, most clearly by Stampa.[1] Many singers and wind players intuitively make use of this counterpressure by the diaphragm, which has the effect, by slowing down the deflation of the lungs, of preventing too much air from being released. It has also been shown that if the tension in the diaphragm slackens, the glottis tends to narrow or even close completely. This is evidently the cause of the background droning sound that can often be heard in wind playing. The breath should always be released easily and smoothly. Equally, breathing in should also always be smooth and without tension or apparent effort.

Leo Kofler[2] distinguishes four types of breathing:

1. Collarbone or shallow breathing (clavicular breathing)
2. Side, chest or rib breathing (costal breathing)
3. Diaphragm/stomach breathing (abdominal breathing)
4. Costal-abdominal breathing

1. is the most unsuitable form of breathing for singers and wind players, since the quantity of air inhaled is necessarily fairly small. This type of breathing can be detected by a raising of the shoulders and the simultaneous retraction of the front abdominal wall.
2. raises the ribs without any protrusion of the stomach muscles.
3. moves only the diaphragm and the ribs. The external signs are a slight expansion of the ribs and a movement of the front abdominal wall.
4. is the best method of breathing for singers and wind players. It is a combination of diaphragm and rib breathing and involves the concerted use of all the respiratory muscles. It should be remembered that inhalation is initiated by a movement of the diaphragm. This ensures that the correct movement of the stomach muscles follows. The reverse sequence – beginning the controlled-breathing process by using the stomach muscles – makes it impossible to obtain much action on the part of the diaphragm.

It is worth giving the average quantities of air breathed in during a full inhalation, using the four different types of breathing:[3]

| Type 1 | 2150 cc |
|--------|---------|
| Type 2 | 3260 cc |
| Type 3 | 2680 cc |
| Type 4 | 3960 cc |

(Average values, men)

The common notion that the amount of air used in playing the recorder is very small is based on a confusion between air quantity and air pressure. The air channel of the recorder is of constant size and does not offer any significant resistance to the air flow. The quantity of air passing through is thus relatively large: 'With the recorder, the expenditure is much greater than it is with the bassoon, hautbois or traversière.'[4] The player of a reed instrument uses high air pressure but a relatively small quantity of air, because the opening between the reeds is narrow. Even the transverse flute can be played with a smaller amount of breath, using normal embouchure in a comfortable register.

*b) Breath support*

Breath support is plainly a vital aspect of correct breathing. It is dealt with here under a separate heading because the concept, although important and often evoked, is not always properly understood. The process is clearly defined by Barth:[5]

> Physiologically speaking, the concept of breath support should be regarded as the sensation which informs us of the respiratory tension of the rib cage in singing and speaking (during exhalation) and which thereby enables us to exercise voluntary control of our use of breath. Once again, the most secure breath support is provided by the costal-abdominal breathing rhythm, in which the respiratory tension is felt both in the pit of the stomach (as a result of the contraction of the diaphragm) and in the walls of the chest.

Even during exhalation, therefore, the downward pressure of the diaphragm does not provide support in the strict sense of the word; it pulls downwards. The term 'support' is thus liable to be a source of confusion. It is more useful to think in terms of diaphragm tension than of a misleading notion of support. It is important for the teacher to avoid using terms which conflict with the correct sequence of physical movements the student should perform. A teacher needs great skill to be able to give proper direction to these movements, which at first are quite untutored. On the other hand, it is certainly not the best course to put the organic processes into the forefront of the student's mind straight away. All of these movements involve tension, and making a student aware of them usually increases the tension further. The teacher must be familiar with all the physical processes, but must steer the student away from excessive self-consciousness, especially during playing. Only later should the movements in the diaphragm and pharynx be discussed, when they have already been developed under careful guidance.

Several different aspects of a wind player's breathing need training: expanding the breath supply, lengthening the process of exhalation, and producing an even breath flow. With recorder playing specifically, any unevenness in the breath flow is directly heard in the form of fluctuations in pitch. Once again, the player's sense of the correct degree of diaphragm tension is vital.

### c) Action of the mouth and pharynx

The pharynx (the top of the throat) consists of three sections. The upper section connects with the nose; the middle section is the rear outlet of the oral cavity; and the lower section – which is of particular significance for singers – is in close proximity to the larynx.

In correct breath production, the nasal cavity is sealed off from the oral cavity by the movement of the soft palate (see diagrams). The soft palate is raised and tensed, so that the oral cavity becomes the only air passage.

Although most wind players create this air passage automatically, some players need to be made aware of this separation of the oral and nasal cavities. The separation of the upper from the middle section of the pharynx, combined with the valve-like closure of the breath passage by the tongue and the exhalatory movement of the thorax and diaphragm, causes the breath to become compressed, thus altering the volume of air. This change in the volume of air in turn causes an increase in atmospheric pressure, which supports the lips from the inside while the instrument is being played. During playing, this pressure can be clearly felt above and below the lip opening. It makes tongue movements become significantly more effective, especially in rapid tonguing and double-tonguing. Indistinct articulation and a nasal tone are often caused by incomplete closure of the nasal cavity.

Schematic diagram of the action of the mouth and throat

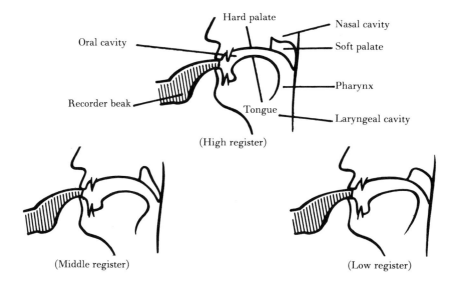

Hard palate

Nasal cavity

Oral cavity

Soft palate

Pharynx

Recorder beak

Tongue

Laryngeal cavity

(High register)

(Middle register)                                        (Low register)

### d) Breath quantity

It is a cardinal principle of many schools of wind playing that the player should breathe as often and as deeply as possible. This rule, however, is quite false. The player must learn early on that the quantity of breath taken in should be dictated by the phrase being played. Breathing in too deeply cramps the diaphragm and interferes with the next outward breath. Acquiring a sense of the length of a phrase is a matter of practice and experience. Regular training of the respiratory muscles gradually increases the breath capacity, so that a breath quantity which would cause tightening in a beginner will later come to seem quite normal.

It should also be stressed that healthy organs are an essential prerequisite of controlled breathing. On the whole, disorders of the heart or the respiratory system make wind playing inadvisable, although if they are not too severe they need not rule it out entirely. Since the process of exhalation is significantly lengthened, however, and since inhalation also calls for considerably more effort than in normal breathing, physical health is vital, at any rate for performing at the highest levels.

Breath technique in wind playing is a consciously trained way of using the respiratory organs that gradually becomes automatic. Even the interaction between the breathing process and the attention the player pays to interpretation can be monitored and, to a certain extent, developed. The level of concentration on interpretation certainly has an effect on the physiological processes that occur in wind playing. Since the ability to concentrate, however, depends on the player's temperament, intelligence and, indeed, character, it cannot in turn really be trained to any great extent.

## Tone

The windway of the recorder is a device expressly built for the purpose of blowing air into the instrument. This is a basic difference between the recorder and its sister instrument, the transverse flute, where the player produces sounds by shaping and directing the air-stream with the lips. This specialized use of the lip and mouth muscles, or embouchure, makes possible great diversity of pitch, dynamics and timbre. With the recorder, the windway of the instrument directs the air-stream on to the labium edge by a prescribed route; the windway, in other words, has the function of the lips in the case of the transverse flute. The variations of timbre obtainable on the recorder are accordingly much more restricted. By the same token, these limited possibilities need to be exploited exhaustively. It is not the purpose of recorder playing to imitate the flute, but the repertoire of pieces for the recorder that has accumulated over several centuries certainly exploits the instrument's own capacities to the full.

The material and method of construction of an instrument play a major role in determining its distinctive tonal qualities. Depending on its method of construction and its condition, a recorder can sound thin or full-bodied, shallow or rounded, nasal or open, husky or clear. Its 'speech' can be virtually free of extraneous noise or have the 'spitting' quality found on early organs. The important thing is to discover the distinctive sound qualities of a particular instrument and tailor one's playing accordingly. Only if these features are carefully studied can the instrument's full tonal possibilities be brought out. This requires more patience and willingness to listen attentively than recorder players are usually given credit for.

The model for recorder sound has always been singing. In the words of Martin Agricola:[6]

> *Wiltu ein Fundament begreiffen*
> *Auff Flöten | Krumhörnern| künstlich pfeiffen*
> *Und auff Zinken | Bomhart | Schalmeyn mit list,*
> *So mercke das volgend zu aller frist.*
>
> *Wiltu ein recht Fundament vberkomen,*
> *So bringt dir der gesang grossen fromen.*
> *Auff den Instrumenten gehts also zu:*
> *Wer den gsang versteht, der mag mit ru*
>
> *Ynn einem halben Quartal (wenn er vleis thut)*
> *Mehr fassen und lernen ym seinem mut,*
> *Als einer des gesangs vnerfahren*
> *Ynn eim halben iar mag ersparen*

(If you wish to understand the foundation of playing skilfully on flutes and crumhorns, and of playing with artistry on the cornett, pommer and shawm, then remember the following at all times. If you desire a true foundation, you will do well to bear singing in mind: if you understand singing, you will certainly learn more about instruments in six weeks (if you are diligent) than someone ignorant of singing will discover in six months)

As with singing, the resonance system of the mouth and pharynx must be activated as well as the sound source proper. Singers are used to regarding the spaces above the larynx (the pharyngeal, oral and nasal cavities) as supplementary to the sound source in the larynx itself and to incorporating them into the process of sound and timbre production. Exploiting these possibilities is similarly an essential ingredient in mastering wind technique. Here it is particularly the increase and decrease in diaphragm tension that has a close bearing on the actions of the upper organs. When the diaphragm is in tension, it pulls down the larynx and holds it in this lower position. This prevents the pharyngeal muscles from tightening, and the vibrating air is thus able to spread freely and react strongly with the resonant cavities of the head. Once again, the teacher should make an effort to get the student to develop the right internal muscular sensations. The more the inhalatory process becomes a matter of sheer willpower, the less the diaphragm is involved, whereas the correct action of the diaphragm is essential for the opening of the pharynx and the extension of the soft palate. A good teacher must be resourceful in suggesting mental aids here. The student can be told, for example, to imagine the air-stream being directed on to the root of the nose and the upper jaw: the mental image of the sound flowing through the upper jaw to the region of the lower lip will draw the student's attention to the role of the resonant cavities of the head. It must always be remembered that mastering an instrument does not consist merely in mastering a technique: it also rests on psychological foundations.

Some modern recorder manuals[7] suggest that the processes of vowel formation can be used in perfecting tone in different registers of the instrument. The player is asked to imagine that he is producing an *o* in the low register, an *a* in the middle register, and an *ü* (as in the German *umlaut*) in the high register. This means that in the low register the soft palate is extended, while remaining somewhat raised; in the middle register it is in the deep position; and in the high register it is raised. These movements cause changes in the oral and pharyngeal cavities which improve tone quality and the instrument's 'speech' (see illustration on p. 24).

Variations in breath pressure produce differences in tone. With higher pressure, the sound becomes shriller and more rasping; with lower pressure, it becomes softer and purer. Either of these options can be used if the music requires it.

An early, detailed discussion of breath quantity and breath pressure can be found in Hieronymus Cardanus's *De musica* of 1546.[8] Cardanus classifies breath quantities as full, shallow and moderate, and breath pressure as relaxed, intense and moderate. As examples he mentions large recorders, the playing style of which must be both full and relaxed, and the horn, where it must be full and intense.

Tonguing has only an indirect bearing on recorder tone, apart from the sounds necessarily involved in initial production and the ugly clicking sounds that are a common feature of faulty tonguing technique. If breath control is good, so that a fine, pure tone quality is produced, then articulation will be clear and vivid; if it is not good, both tone and articulation will be insipid and lacking in character.

An important means of creating tonal variety is vibrato. Vibrato is fundamental to singing and wind playing and is closely connected with the role of the diaphragm in the breathing process. In the ancient world the diaphragm was held to be the seat of the soul, and the use of diaphragm vibrato was a natural outgrowth of the theory of the emotions. When used in the right place and with sensitivity, vibrato adds vitality and sheen to the voice and to wind tone. Technically speaking, it is produced by a series of vibrations of the diaphragm, of greater or lesser rapidity, which produce variations of pressure in the outgoing air-stream. The speed (frequency) and size (amplitude) of the vibrato can vary, producing differences of tone. Sounds with vibrato are also different in quality from those without vibrato, and may be deliberately juxtaposed for contrastive effect. The 'trembling breath' described by Agricola[9] and the 'unusual *gratia*' which Praetorius[10] observed as resulting from this change of voice quality are clear evidence of an awareness of the role of the diaphragm in producing head and chest resonance. Marin Mersenne[11] describes 'certain vibrations which intoxicate the mind'. He says that the frequency of the organ tremulant is four vibrations per second: the wind player's choice of fine gradations of vibrato is superior to this. According to Geminiani (*c.*1750), vibrato may be applied to each note; on the other hand (cf. Rousseau, Mersenne and Ganassi), exaggerated, uniformly rapid or uninterrupted vibrato is frowned upon. The character, style and instrumentation of a piece will determine the amount and type of vibrato that should be applied. A late-baroque solo sonata, with its subjective mode of expression, needs to be played with more vibrato than a fifteenth-century ensemble piece.

Further gradations of tone can be produced by special fingerings. So-called '*piano* fingerings' – fingerings which are too sharp, but which are to be played softly to adjust the intonation – are not only softer than normally fingered notes but also different in timbre. Other shadings of tone colour can be produced by the reverse procedure: namely, gently covering an extra finger-hole while blowing more loudly to compensate for the difference in pitch.

Many cross-fingerings produce a more muted sound than those produced by normal fingerings. The result is that scales can be non-uniform in tone, though not as markedly as on the baroque flauto traverso. These tonal disparities, which of course are particularly audible in keys with several accidentals, are often deliberately exploited by the composer. In contemporary music, finger vibrato, variable speeds of diaphragm vibrato and new vibrato effects have also been used.[12]

A final way of obtaining a wider range of timbre is to use more than one type of instrument. The width and taper of the bore are the main relevant factors here. It is desirable to alternate between, say, a high-baroque and a Renaissance recorder, or a softer-toned and harsher-toned instrument, depending on the music involved and taking full account of the tonal differences between the instruments.

## Posture

The chief precept as far as playing posture is concerned is: relax! The muscles of the neck and throat, particularly, should consciously be kept loose. Unnecessary muscular tensions affect other groups of muscles and lead to general tightening-up. Controlled breathing is the key to good posture, and diaphragm tension is the key to all other bodily movements. If the diaphragm tension is correct, then the proper movements of the other muscles will fall into place; if it is insecure, the body will compensate by over-straining the skeletal muscles. This in turn leads to cramp, which impairs performance.

The feet should not be too close together: if the legs are apart, the body can move freely in sympathy with the music. It is advisable to take most of the weight on one leg, allowing the other leg, slightly advanced, to cushion and balance the movements of the body. If you are playing sitting down, you should again make sure you can feel that your body is relaxed. The head should be held straight, not lowered or tilted to one side. Sit on the front part of the chair, not leaning against the back; the small of the back should not droop. The motto, 'Head up, shoulders down', helps ensure a good, relaxed posture.

Many players, consciously or unconsciously, underline the musical expression in a piece by making vigorous bodily movements. This is a bad habit, not only visually unattractive but also an obstacle to relaxed breathing and good finger work. Occasional practice in front of the mirror is a good antidote.

The recorder should be held about 30 cm (12 inches) away from the body. To avoid cramping the rib cage, make sure that the arms are not held too closely adjacent to the body, but are angled slightly outwards. Holding the instrument too high is not only unsightly but makes the arms too tense. The recorder should be inserted between the lips in a straight line directly beneath the root of the nose. The lips enclose the top part of the recorder beak entirely, but without tension. It is extremely important not to let any air escape by not fully closing the lips. This fault – especially common with beginners – significantly alters the air pressure in the oral cavity and reduces the weight of the sound, making it weak and nasal, particularly in the overblown octave.

The fingers should be placed flat against the instrument, so that the pads of the fingers, not the tips, cover the holes. It is important not to exaggerate the raising and lowering of the fingers, and the finger-holes should be closed without undue pressure. The finger movements are made from the finger joints and should not extend back up the arm. There is a tendency to make big, forced movements in difficult passages; students should be taught to resist this temptation. Occasional practice of vigorous tapping finger movements can be useful for building up control in difficult fingering sequences, but heavy finger movements accompanied by obvious tapping noises are a common error and should be avoided completely.

A sense of the proper balance of the recorder as it is held in playing position helps ensure that the movements of the fingers are at once relaxed and

Holding the recorder: illustration from *traversière* Hotteterre, *Principes de la Flûte* [...], 1707

Alternative hand positions, from Virdung, *Musica getutscht und ausgezogen*, 1511

precise. The lips (particularly the lower lip) and the right thumb support the instrument; further support is given by the fingers of the left hand. A properly positioned recorder is kept in equilibrium by the lips, the left middle finger and the supporting right thumb, so that it is impossible for the instrument to slip loose. The other fingers should provide only the minimum of extra support necessary. Some extra support is often unavoidable, of course, when passing from the lower octave to the overblown higher octave. For this it is best to use the little finger of the right hand, resting it on the beading between the instrument's middle and foot joints. Using other fingers to provide support can easily impede smooth sequences of movement (see also 'supporting finger technique', p. 35).

## Methods of fingering

The way an instrument should be fingered depends on the exact nature of its bore. Even with recorders built in basically the same way, slight variations in fingering are necessary as a result of small differences in bore. But there are also fundamentally different kinds of bore, and radically different methods of fingering as a result. We can distinguish baroque, English and German fingering methods.

The terms 'baroque' and 'English' are often used interchangeably. Strictly speaking, the term 'baroque' should be confined to exact replicas of the early fingering systems. The English method is based broadly on baroque fingerings but differs from most of the sets of instructions that have survived. The main differences concern the fourth degree of the scale and its upper octave (on the f′ treble recorder, the notes b′ flat and b″ flat) and the sharpened octave above the instrument's lowest note (f″ sharp on the f′ treble recorder).

Until recently the German fingering system constituted an alternative to the baroque/English method. This system arose in the 1920s, as the result of a misunderstanding. Peter Harlan, in building a copy of an early instrument, altered what he believed to be a 'bad' fingering for the fourth degree of the scale. In his new fingering system this note was produced by the right index finger alone, rather than by a cross-fingering. This simplified fingering, however, while apparently insignificant in itself, was achieved at a cost, since the overblown sharpened fourth degree of the scale was now too sharp, and there were further problems of intonation with semitone intervals.

Only a recorder with baroque fingering, therefore, is suitable for advanced purposes. There has also been a gradual shift away from the view that the German fingering system is easier for beginners. Defenders of the German system maintain that it is very difficult to teach children the cross-fingering for the fourth degree of the scale. Against this, however, it can be said

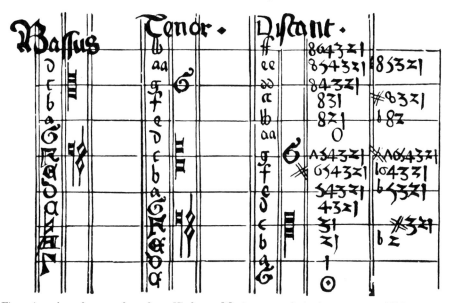

Fingering chart for recorders, from Virdung, *Musica getutscht und ausgezogen*, 1511

Ayre for recorder, with fingerings, from Robert Carr, *The Delightful Companion*, 1686

that it is merely a matter of good teaching practice to wait until the right moment before the fingering is introduced. In any case, fingering problems on the recorder are not confined to this fingering alone: playing the instrument involves a range of different cross-fingerings, in varying combinations.

From earliest times, fingering charts outlining the whole range of possible fingerings were included in instruction books. In these charts the covering fingers are indicated by numerals (Virdung, Agricola), letters (Cardanus) or solid and open circles (Ganassi,[13] Blanckenburgh,[14] Hotteterre[15]). Given the nature of the instrument, these fingerings have been basically similar in all periods. The main differences concern compass, the number of chromatic notes given, and the number of alternative and trill fingerings. Surviving charts contain the following compasses and numbers of specified fingerings:

|  | Compass (in degrees of the scale) | Number of diatonic/ chromatic fingerings | Total |
|---|---|---|---|
| Sebastian Virdung 1511 | I–VII' | 14/8 | 22 |
| Martin Agricola 1528/45 | I–VII' | 15/9 | 24 |
| Sylvestro Ganassi 1535 | I–VI' | 14/10 | 24 |
| Hieronymus Cardanus 1546 | I–III" | 17/6 | 23 |

| | | | |
|---|---|---|---|
| Martin Mersenne 1636 | I–I" | 15/4 | 19 |
| Gerbrandt van Blanckenburgh 1654 | I–II" | 16/20 | 36 |
| Jacques Hotteterre le Romain 1707 | I–I" | 16/10 | 26 |
| *The Modern Music Master c.*1731 | I–I" | 15/11 | 26 |
| J. F. B. C. Majer 1732[16] | I–IV" | 18/12 | 30 |
| Thomas Stanesby Junior *c.*1732[17] | I–II" | 16/31 | 47 |

In the last analysis, intonation is a matter of individual judgement. A player can use variations both in fingering and in breath-pressure to alter the tuning of the instrument as desired, albeit within limits.

Unequal temperament gives rise to differences between enharmonic notes. The note E flat, for example, is played one comma sharper than D sharp (one 'Telemann comma' sharper, i.e. 1/55 of an octave), and D sharp is very slightly flattened. Considerations of this sort are widely discussed in early treatises, but are not always spelled out with precision into diagrammatic fingering charts and verbal fingering instructions. As far as the recorder is concerned, Blanckenburgh was probably the first author to make a distinction between notes marked with a ♯ and those marked with a ♭. The first equivalent distinctions for the transverse flute are to be found in Hotteterre. Blanckenburgh obtains these intonational distinctions by means of separate fingerings, but the differences are very fine ones. Hotteterre distinguishes the enharmonic notes on the transverse flute mainly by prescribing differences in embouchure, where the degree of alteration can naturally be very variable. With the recorder, by contrast, the instructions involve fingerings in which the holes are either slightly more, or slightly less, than half covered, so that the degree of difference in intonation is again extremely subtle. As far as Johann Joachim Quantz is concerned, the enharmonic distinctions remain valid – he points out, for example, that G flat is sharper on all instruments than F sharp – but this does not, he says, apply to the '*Clavier*', which must have a 'good temperament' in order that the two semitones may sound 'tolerable'.[18] There was clearly a problem here. When playing a work involving a keyboard instrument, the wind player had to aim for a midway position so that tuning could be consistent. This implies that a distinction was made between the intonation used in solo pieces and that required in works with accompaniment. In any case, there were conflicting views concerning the importance of temperament. Corette says:[19] 'It is true that D sharp and E flat are not exactly the same; but the difference is so excessively small that there is no reason why time should be spent attempting to find it on the flute.' Nevertheless, despite this dissident opinion, traditionally minded authors retained for a considerable time the method of systematically distinguishing enharmonic notes. As far as the transverse flute is concerned, it was not until Devienne[20] that the issue was resolved in favour of a system of well-tempered tuning, albeit one in which D sharp, for example, was pitched lower if functioning as a third than as the leading note. Of the surviving fingering charts for the recorder, only Thomas Stanesby's (*c.*1732) gives a systematic set of different fingerings for enharmonic notes. His specifications relate to his preferred instrument, the tenor recorder:

Stanesby, 'A Scale in C, for the Flute à bec, or Common English Flute'

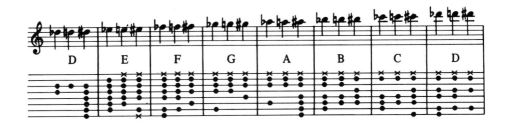

A number of early instruction books also specify trill fingerings. The first detailed account is in Ganassi, covering trills of a whole tone, semitone and third. Cardanus provides further refinements (combinations of alternative fingerings with changes in breath-pressure), and Hotteterre later offers a comprehensive summary. Using charts, Hotteterre distinguishes between *tremblements ou cadences* (trills with the upper auxiliary note) and *pincés ou battements* (mordents with the lower auxiliary). (See also *flattement*, p. 112.) Many of the fingerings he gives are based on the fact that trills are more effective if the upper note is fingered slightly sharp:

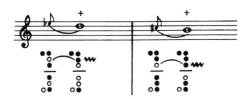

Quantz also mentions this phenomenon. He recommends starting the trill with a single correct interval, but continuing it by fingering it too sharp while using gentler breath-pressure.

Hotteterre's general method of fingering is a systematic extension of a method used earlier by Mersenne. It is a 'supporting finger technique', in which the third (ring) finger of the right hand is kept down for most notes. This certainly gives the instrument good support, but the switching from supported to unsupported notes that results merely gives rise to new problems. In addition, on many recorders the use of supporting finger technique causes distortions of intonation. For these reasons the method has never really become established.

Cardanus, in his concern to enlarge the recorder's playing potential, offers some extensions to conventional fingering technique. He demonstrates how the instrument can be leant against the leg so that the sound-hole in the foot joint is either partly or wholly covered. This has the effect of altering the pitch and increasing the compass (downwards). He also mentions the possibility of using a key (or virgula) for the lowest finger-hole. Hitherto keys had been mentioned only in connection with the bass recorder (by Agricola).

A thorough comparative study of thirty-one well-known and less well-known fingering charts[21] shows a very complex picture. There are differences even among fingering systems of the same period. One important fact to emerge is that double holes for the two lowest notes were not common. As a result, we find fingerings such as these:

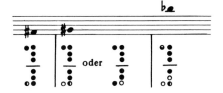

These fingerings produce uneven successions of tone colours. It should be added, however, that Hotteterre, for example, when explaining trill fingerings, does specify alternatives 'si le trou est double'.

Unequal temperament necessarily entailed variations in fingering, with the player making adjustments in accordance with his sense of pitch. Then as now, the instrument maker merely produced a basic general tuning. No wind instrument has a single, clear-cut and unambiguous tuning; the player always needs to make corrections. In addition, it should be remembered that the recorder – as Quantz says of the transverse flute – has its 'natural faults' of intonation. A player should never hide behind the excuse of his instrument's tuning if it is his own intonation that is amiss. Still less can we speak of an 'old fingering system' pure and simple and use it to attack the standard modern ('baroque') system as new and, for that reason, stylistically dubious.

## Fingering technique

### a) Silent finger exercises

The shape and size of the fingers are less critical for wind players than for string players. Nevertheless, slim and mobile fingers are particularly suitable, while short, thick, inflexible fingers are a drawback. Special exercises can be used to reduce or eliminate general and localized stiffness in the fingers. Most people find that their two hands have very different degrees of facility, especially as regards the ability to perform controlled sequences of movement with the fingers. Generally speaking, the left hand, which is used less often in daily life, performs less well than the right.

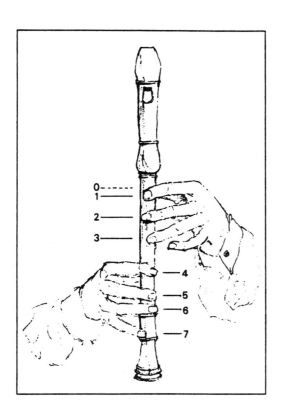

The different fingers of the same hand also have varying degrees of facility. The thumb is strong but awkward (in recorder playing only the left thumb is active). The index and middle fingers are the most naturally mobile. The little finger is less mobile than the index and middle fingers, but more so than the thumb. The third (ring) finger is the weakest physiologically and the most restricted. Finger exercises should take these different capacities into account.

In the following silent finger exercises,[22] the chief rule is to relax and not exaggerate the movements. As soon as the fingers begin to tire, drop the arms and relax so that their weight can really be felt. Gentle massage between the knuckles will relieve any tension. The exercises are intended as suggestions; they can be varied in any number of ways at the player's discretion.

Parallel movements
(simultaneous raising and lowering in both hands)

|  | left | right |
|---|---|---|
| One finger | 1 | 4 |
|  | 2 | 5 |
|  | 3 | 6 |
|  | 0 | 7 |
| Two fingers at a time | 1/2 | 4/5 |
| (each hand separately, then together) | 1/3 | 4/6 |
|  | 1/0 | 4/7 |
|  | 2/3 | 5/6 |
|  | 2/0 | 5/7 |
| One finger vs. two | 1 | 4/5 |
|  | 2 | 4/5 etc. |
|  | 1 | 5/6 |
|  | 2 | 5/6 etc. |
|  | 1 | 6/7 |
|  | 2 | 6/7 etc. |

| Contrary movement (raising in one hand and lowering in the other) | left (raising) | right (lowering) |
|---|---|---|
| | 1 | 4 |
| | 1 | 5 |
| | 1 | 6 |
| | 1 | 7 |
| | 2 | 4 |
| | 2 | 5 etc. |
| | 1 | 4/5 |
| | 1 | 5/6 |
| | 1 | 6/7 |
| | 1 | 5/7 (keep 6 down) |
| | 2 | 4/5 |
| | 2 | 4/6 |
| | 2 | 4/7 |
| | | (keep 5 and 6 down) |
| | 2 | 5/6 |
| | 2 | 5/7 |
| | 2 | 6/7 |
| | 3 | 4/5 |
| | 3 | 4/6 |
| | 3 | 4/7 |
| | 3 | 5/6 |
| | 3 | 5/7 |
| | 3 | 6/7 |

| Combined (contrary movement and contrary direction) | left | right |
|---|---|---|
| | 1 | 5 |
| | 2 | 6 |
| | 3 | 7 |
| | 0 | 4 |
| | 2 | 4 |
| | 3 | 5 |
| | 0 | 6 |
| | 1 | 7 |

| | |
|---|---|
| 1 | 6 |
| 2 | 7 |
| 3 | 4 |
| 0 | 5 |

| | |
|---|---|
| 3 | 4 |
| 0 | 5 |
| 1 | 6 |
| 2 | 7 etc. |

## b) Technique

Below are some basic exercises that can be used for practising standard fingering problems. Obviously, the variations are limitless and new exercises can easily be worked out. You should make a point of turning even the smallest technical exercise into a piece of music: it should have a clearly marked beginning and a well-shaped ending.

i) Scales (chromatic scales to be practised similarly)
Short scale exercise

Long scale exercise

ii) Broken chords
Four patterns (other broken chords to be practised similarly)

I

II

III

IV

iii) Combinations of scales and broken chords (diatonic)

iv) Intervals based on scales (including chromatic scales)

Points to watch:

1. Start scales and broken chords on the lowest triadic note, going up to the highest (e.g. in the B flat major scale, from f′ to f″).
2. Practise all exercises with different styles of articulation.

Special exercises involving broken triads and chains of sevenths, pentatonic patterns, abbreviated sequences etc. are included in some teaching manuals.[23]

Technical exercises should be played by heart. This will make you more aware of any problems, and it also means that what you learn is eventually absorbed by the unconscious, where it can be drawn on at the required moment. Finger movements should be relaxed and not exaggerated. Thomas Mace wrote in 1676:[24] 'I used to compare such Tossing-Finger'd-Players, to Blind-Horses, which always lift up their Feet, Higher than need is; and so by that means, can never Run Fast, or with a Smooth Swiftness: It is therefore, both Commendable, and Profitable, to Play Close ...'

Particular attention should be paid to the following special problems, for which appropriate exercises should be worked out:

Low register/high register
Thumb technique; exercises for leaps
Movements with groups of fingers; legato exercises
Non-legato/portato or staccato
Portato/legato or non-legato

*c) Exercises based on passages from pieces*

The following suggestions may be of help when you are faced with a technically difficult passage in a particular piece. (Of course, there is no single and obligatory way of interpreting the passage in a musical sense.)

Let us take as an example a passage from the Brandenburg Concerto No. 4 by J. S. Bach (first movement, bars 165–7):

i) Difficult note-groups can be practised separately, and you can also practise the transition from one group to the next:

ii) The figure can be practised in different rhythms:

iii) And with different patterns of articulation:

The vital thing is to identify the different elements in a difficult passage and put in extra work on those elements that need it. It is best to practise a passage slowly at first and build up speed gradually. Do not be afraid to use a metronome if it helps.

Some further suggestions for practice include:
  a) Fingering the notes silently (without producing a sound), concentrating solely on the finger movements.
  b) Practising fingerings for each hand separately.

c) Separating the finger movements from tonguing, in a regular rhythm:

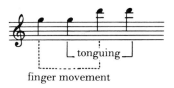

## *Articulation*

Articulation in music is the way in which the individual notes in a note sequence are 'enunciated': in other words, the way in which they are joined to, or separated from, one another. Phrasing, by contrast, is the process whereby the structure of a melody is brought out, either at a local or at a wider level. According to Hermann Keller, a leading authority on the question, phrasing is concerned with 'what I say', while articulation is concerned with 'how I say it'.[25]

In their method of sound production, wind instruments are most closely akin to the human voice. As with the voice, sounds are articulated by means of interruptions and resumptions of the air-stream. Articulation on the recorder consists in the contrasting use of tongued and slurred notes. The tongue acts like a valve, blocking the outward flow of the air-stream when placed gently against the alveolar ridge in front of the hard palate and freeing it again when withdrawn (see illustration below). While this happens, the sides of the tongue rest quietly against both rows of upper molars, so that only the tip of the tongue actually moves. Cultivating a sense of this delicate movement by the tip of the tongue is essential in learning to articulate with precision. If the tonguing movement comes from the root of the tongue, small blockages of air are created which severely hamper the evenness of the air flow. If too wide an area of the tongue is used, clicking sounds can easily occur.

Exactly how the tongue should be applied depends on the shape of the tongue itself. Ideally it should be flat, mobile and neither too long nor too wide. If it is very large, it will be less mobile because it will always rub against the teeth, particularly the upper ones. It is possible to tell even from the way someone speaks that his tongue may be unsuitable for recorder playing: clear lisping on *s*-sounds is a case in point, as is a pushing of the tongue against the front teeth on the consonants *t* and *d*. Tongue movements of this kind make for blurred articulation and also put a strain on the tongue, which is liable to tire in any case. Along with good breathing, relaxed and flexible tonguing is the secret of successful wind technique.

Correct tonguing position                    Incorrect tonguing position

This brief discussion indicates that the tongue muscles are of paramount importance in securing precision in the initiation of a musical sound. The genioglossus muscle begins at the inner side of the lower jaw, sending fibres fanwise up into the tip of the tongue and branching out into the root in the other direction. The closing-off of the air-stream, and hence the tonguing process, begins with this muscle. Several other muscles are also involved, including the geniohyoid muscle, the effect of which can most easily be seen externally (in the area of the chin and throat) when it is operating in tandem with the genioglossus above it to produce the movement known as double-tonguing. Too much visible movement in this area shows that the root of the tongue is making too much effort. Ideally, tonguing should place as little strain on the tongue muscles as possible, while securing the desired effect. Accordingly, the normal place at which tongue contact should occur is slightly above and behind the incisors. If the tongue touches the teeth, or is curved back sharply against the hard palate, its mobility is severely restricted.

Recorder notes should be closed by the tongue with a silent *t*, to prevent the sound from falling away at the end. A played note may thus be represented by the syllable *dü-(t)*. The way in which the tongue initiates or concludes the note determines whether the sound is hard or soft and long or short, and whether it is heard as a separate entity or as linked to one or more other notes. Rounding off a note with a powerful counter-movement of the diaphragm, or by quickly removing the instrument from the lips, should be done rarely: these are not normal methods of articulation.

The four principal styles of articulation on the recorder are as follows:

Non-legato

The notes are slightly separated from one another, in other words shortened by about one-third or a quarter of their value. Non-legato articulation is the normal type of articulation on the recorder.

If two or more notes are connected by a slur, only the first is tongued and only the last is closed by the tongue.

The breath flow is sustained as with a long note, and is interrupted only by a light tonguing movement without pressure. The tongue movement that ends one note is coextensive with the tonguing that starts the next note. The smaller and briefer the tongue movement, the closer the link between the two notes.

The tongue leaves the alveolar ridge very briefly before closing off the air-stream again. The quicker the tongue movement, the shorter the note. The duration of staccato notes is determined not by their notated values, but by the (variable) length of the resulting brief rests.

The wealth of finer gradations of articulation which go to make up a musical performance cannot be captured in notation. They are produced, however, by modifications of the main types outlined in schematic form here.

'Double-tonguing' is a distinctive method of articulation, used for rapid staccato sequences of notes. Its main application on the recorder is in the range between the notes c″ and d‴, since the highest and lowest notes in the compass respond poorly when played with double-tonguing. The tip and back of the tongue alternate to give the syllables *dik* and *ke*. It should be noted that the closing *k* of the first syllable, which replaces what would be the usual closing *t* (i.e. *di-(t)*), is not articulated separately, but cuts off the air-stream silently and is coextensive with the initial *k* of the second syllable. These articulatory syllables have to be produced so far forward in the mouth that the *k* almost becomes a *g*. (For Quantzian double-tonguing, see p. 104.)

In rapid dotted rhythms the following type of tonguing can be used:

dü(t)    dü - rü(t)    dü(t)    dü - rü(t)    ‖.    dü(t)    dü - rü(t)    dü - rü(t)    dü .....

Whether the dot of the dotted note is held or is realized as a brief rest depends on the length of the first syllable. The syllable *rü* begins with a sound roughly between a *d* and a rolled *r*.

In flutter-tonguing the breath flow is kept constant while the tongue produces a very rapid, sustained rolled *r* in the front of the mouth. Sometimes, depending on the shape of the player's mouth and position of the teeth, it can be produced with a uvular *r* (at the back of the mouth). Breath-pressure is greater in flutter-tonguing than in normal tonguing, as the tongue impedes the air-stream.

Patterns of articulation can be converted into sequences of syllables and practised as speech exercises. Thus the articulatory sequence:

can be represented by the syllabic sequence:

*düt düt dü-(t), dü-(t)_dü-(t)_dü-(t), düt düt dü-(t)_düt dü-(t)_düt dü-(t).*

(For further discussion of articulatory syllables in the historical literature, see pp. 63ff. and 102ff.)

Co-ordination between the muscles of the mouth and tongue is impossible if there is any tension or cramping. If the mouth muscles are tensed, the tongue muscles will inevitably become strained too, and uncertain, clumsy sounds will result. Tensions in these upper muscles can spread down as far as the chest.

The function of the mylohyoid muscle and the digastric muscle is to pull down the lower jaw. When used correctly, these muscles create the necessary gap between the upper and lower teeth to allow the air-stream to pass through. Pulling the jaw too far down, however, stops the free play of all the muscles used in the breathing process. The only time any significant dropping of the jaw is possible is in a very delicate portato, when the oral cavity is very arched. Excessive strain on these muscles is particularly likely to occur if the head is lowered – but this is very poor posture in any case.

Brass players, flautists and oboists make considerable use of the orbicularis oris around the mouth: it is the principal muscle used in sound production by trombonists, for example. It has a much smaller role in recorder playing, however. Its effect is to bring the cheeks into light contact with the upper set of molars and incisors. This prevents air particles from gathering in the front part of the oral cavity, where they can interfere with sound production. Puffing out the cheeks can often lead to an uneven breath flow.

The size and shape of the teeth, similarly, are less significant in recorder playing than they are with brass instruments. Nevertheless, players with particularly large upper incisors may have difficulty in making the air flow unimpeded through the teeth into the windway of the instrument. In cases of overbite (protruding upper jaw and upper teeth) the upper lip should be placed over the teeth so that the teeth do not bear down on the recorder beak. A very pronounced overbite, or very large incisors, will cause a considerable amount of tension and make playing difficult.

## Practice

The art of practising properly consists in using the minimum amount of time and energy necessary to achieve the maximum improvement of performance. Practice is itself a special technique, and the technique can gradually be learned. Guidance by the teacher is particularly important here. You should practise in a well-ventilated room, one which is if anything too cool rather than too warm. A daily practice session is best divided into (a) tonal exercises, (b) technical exercises, (c) study work and (d) pieces for performance.

The following brief summary of rules for practice lists the main factors that will help to make your practice profitable.

1. Practise regularly – daily if at all possible.
2. The length of practice time can vary, depending on your stamina, talent, available time etc.
3. Keep practising only while you are still really fresh.
4. If you practise sitting down, bring the hips back, let the shoulders fall slightly, and arch the chest forward (but again only slightly).
5. At intervals – including while you are playing – make a deliberate point of relaxing. Pains in the neck, arm or wrist are a sign that your posture is wrong.
6. Check your finger movements mentally, not by eye.
7. Learn all technical studies by heart.
8. It is better to play a passage forty-nine times slowly and once at speed than vice versa.
9. Never repeat a technical mistake – track down its source straight away and correct it.
10. Jotting down points on your copy will help to guide you in your practice. Signs for articulation and dynamics are not the only ones: all sorts of shorthand markings are useful. Here is a brief list:

| | |
|---|---|
| V | breath |
| (V) | optional breath |
| V | especially deep breath |
| , | caesura made by articulation |
| —— | do not breathe |
| ↑ ↓ | sharper; flatter |
| ⌇ | continuation/transition |
| ◯ | difficult passage |
| N | normal fingering |
| II | alternative (secondary) fingering |
| T | thumbed F sharp |
| ⌐ ¬ | *piano* (echo) phrase |

## Performance

The first worry of every recorder player performing in a larger ensemble is: will I be heard? You should therefore be all the more wary of forcing the sound. The larynx must not be allowed to become constricted through nervous tension, but should be held in a low position by means of good diaphragm control.

The recorder player must face the audience. If you play into your music, you will rob the instrument of sonority.

To counteract nerves, remember the rule: 'Head up, shoulders down'. Take deep breaths during rests and consciously relax the whole body, especially the fingers. Even while you are playing you can loosen the area of the shoulders and back of the neck. The head should remain mobile: it needs 'room for manoeuvre'. The bigger the room or hall in which you are playing, the clearer you need to make the beginnings and ends of slurred phrases, the crisper your tonguing, and the steadier your tempo. In a large hall, vibrato should err on the side of being too large rather than too small.

For peace of mind, note down performance instructions in the score. These annotations should include a good number of reserve breath-marks, since a badly ventilated or over-heated room will be more taxing on the breath – to say nothing of the tensions produced by performing before an audience.

## Instruction books and studies

In the instruction books of the sixteenth century, directions on recorder playing are given alongside directions for playing other instruments. The recorder belonged to the category of 'miscellaneous instruments' which were either interchangeable among themselves or could be played simultaneously. Instrumental teaching was so much a part of general musical instruction and activity that authors of treatises took it for granted that many points would be explained orally. Agricola, for example, instead of explaining the principles of ornamentation, is content to say:[26] 'You may learn these from a flute player.' As part of this tradition, instruction books were often cast in the form of a dialogue between teacher and pupil. Sebastian Virdung, for example, explains to his apt pupil Andreas Sylvanus what he needs to know regarding the number of finger-holes, finger positions, fingering technique and the use of the tongue. The works of Virdung and his contemporaries are more in the nature of general manuals of musicianship and go less thoroughly into specialized questions involving the recorder itself. Ganassi's manual specifically devoted to the flute is an exception, yet even here more space is given to ornamentation than to matters of technique. Ganassi's relatively large number of technical directions, however, accompanied by music examples, demonstrates beyond dispute how high the standard of recorder playing was during this period. Cardanus's book (1546) is especially notable for its account of varying styles of tone production and for giving special fingerings to increase the compass and alter the pitch. These works, together with those by Agricola (1528/45), Blancken-

Frontispiece from Ganassi, *La Fontegara*, 1535

burgh (1654) and Jambe de Fer (1556), [27] provide vital information on breathing technique and tone production, finger technique, ornamentation and questions of instrumentation. The comparatively brief treatise by Bismantova (1667) describes types of articulation specific to the recorder, clearly distinguished from corresponding instructions for the cornett.[28] Jacques Hotteterre's famous pedagogic work of 1709, the model for several later imitations, contains essential information on playing the *flûte à bec*. Hotteterre gives instructions on articulation, rules for ornaments and fingering charts, both for the recorder specifically and – when a similar playing method is involved – for the *flûte traversière*. In the last important teaching work of the later baroque period, the *Versuch* by Johann Joachim Quantz (1752),[29] the two types of flute are no longer seen as on a par, and only the transverse flute is dealt with in the section on playing method. Many points concerning the recorder, however, can be gleaned from the discussion, and the more extensive section of the work, which is devoted to the performance of the music of the period, contains general rules of interpretation that are also obviously relevant to the recorder.

All told, then, the number of pedagogic works specifically devoted to the recorder is not great. Information on playing technique has been compiled not only from these works but also from the whole range of early writings on the performance of music generally. This is the basis on which the modern approach to recorder playing is founded.

The rediscovery of the recorder in the second decade of the twentieth century has resulted in the publication of a large number of new books on recorder method. Since 1950, in particular, there has been a flood of new titles, in many languages. There are instruction methods for all four main members of the recorder family, although the great majority are for treble and descant. Despite the fact that many of the problems these works discuss are peculiar to the recorder and have therefore already been treated in the historical literature, these modern methods are very variable in their aims and approaches. They can be divided into two groups: methods for beginners, and books for more advanced players.

The most interesting beginners' methods are those which, as well as providing specific instrumental teaching, also incorporate the elements of musical theory. Some publications leave theory out altogether. In others, however, theory is so much to the fore that the recorder becomes merely a means to the end of explaining the basic principles of music. Introducing the learner to musical notation is often a prime concern. The result is that questionable or even absurd suggestions about playing are given, merely because they will be more easily understood. Beginners' methods explicitly geared to group tuition are fairly rare, but the same range of approaches can be found with them.

Within the second group of publications, for advanced players, the prime concern is usually instrumental performance. Historical performance practice, which is naturally a vital topic as far as the recorder is concerned, is covered in varying degrees of depth. Some manuals concentrate on a historical approach, to the complete exclusion of contemporary music, which has now become so important.

The most useful instructional works for the recorder are those which attempt to combine a historically based approach with a contemporary musical perspective. It is quite possible to combine these approaches at different levels of technical difficulty. Perhaps the most important criterion in assessing the quality of these works is the care they take over technical questions specific to wind playing (tone production, articulation, intonation etc.) and over matters of performance practice, both early and modern. In addition, a good teaching text should include a representative selection from the literature and adequate practice material and technical exercises. Last, but certainly not least, it must stimulate and reinforce pleasure in music-making.[30]

Other publications deal with the particular problems of ensemble playing and contain ensemble exercises, from duets upwards.[31] There are also collections of exercises devoted primarily to general matters of technique (e.g. developing speed in fingering and tonguing)[32] or to performance in particular styles within early or contemporary music.[33]

This survey of the wealth of published study material may well make the boundaries between the different types of publication look more clear-cut than they really are. The recorder player is best advised to try to identify and compare the different aspects of the study material available and to select those works which are best suited to his needs. Since these needs vary so greatly from player to player, we shall not offer a list of study materials here; such a list would anyway inevitably be incomplete. Those titles which have been cited are merely a small, personal selection.

# 3

## Recorder Music and its Performance

### The recorder before 1600

*a) The early Middle Ages*

The recorder is an ancient instrument. It was probably used in the folk music of prehistoric southern and western Europe, and it is still in use as an original folk instrument in some countries today.[1] Surviving instruments from antiquity are, of course, extremely rare and are in such a poor state of preservation that they are very difficult even to identify. Virtually no instruments survive from the Middle Ages either. Research sources on medieval instruments therefore consist almost exclusively of pictorial and written records. These records, however, are plentiful and provide much information on the uses to which the recorder was put. All the evidence clearly goes to show that the functions of the recorder were always varied. It was used as a solo instrument and in groups; in purely instrumental ensembles; as an instrument to accompany singers; and as a substitute for the voice. Even though a different function tended to predominate in each period, alternative uses of the instrument were not excluded. The great versatility of the recorder meant that it was held in high esteem for many hundreds of years.

Brought into the West as a shepherd's pipe, the recorder had spread by the early Middle Ages to the lowly social ranks of the minstrels and jongleurs. For a long time, even after it had risen into the more genteel realms of art music and courtly music, it remained a particular emblem – like all pipe instruments – of minstrels, jugglers and acrobats. According to Simone di Golino Prudenziani (1355–1440),[2] 'on the Tuscan estate of one Pierbaldo, the company is entertained for the eight days of Christmas by the acrobat Solazzi. He sings, he plays the viol, the harp, the organ, the flute, the shawm, the psaltery [...]' The music of the minstrels[3] was almost always purely instrumental. The actual choice of instruments was, of course, left quite open, as indeed remained the case generally until the seventeenth century, when composers first began to give explicit instructions about instrumentation. Minstrel music, like most of the music of the minnesingers and trouvères, is monophonic. (The songs of the trouvères can also be performed instrumentally.) The use of instruments in alternation was also possible, as was playing *colla parte* (the instrument doubling at the octave if necessary). Dance music was particularly the minstrels' province. A considerable number of monophonic minstrel dances have survived, the principal kinds being the estampie, the saltarello, the trotto and the rotta. These pieces were often accompanied by a bourdon bass of open fifths. Although the minstrels were not 'respectable' members of society, they also made an important contribution to performances of religious plays. Five hundred minstrels are said to have been employed at the Council of Constance in 1414, playing flutes, vielles and rottas. The art of *diminutio* or improvised organa applied to song melodies was very popular, and accompaniments in thirds make occasional appearances as early as the thirteenth century. We may quote the following comment on the standard of recorder playing in about 1350:[4] 'There has been a change in pipes and pipeplaying: this music has risen higher, and was never as good as it is now. Someone who was thought on all sides to be a good piper five or six years ago is now not worth a fly.'

### b) *Ars Antiqua*

The era of the growth of mensural polyphony in northern France, which can be taken as the period between about 1230 and 1320, is known as the period of the Ars Antiqua. In place of the more approximate neumatic notation that had been used hitherto, notation is now mensural and depicts the relative rhythmic and metrical values of the notes. The music of the Ars Antiqua is predominantly tied to the liturgy, its chief forms being conductus, organum and the motet. The works of the period, often written in three and four parts, represent an important new extension of polyphony. Polyphonic music was regarded as particularly solemn and was performed for special celebratory purposes on the most important days in the religious calendar. These works are 'solistic music composed for professional musicians':[5] the doxological function of the music is enhanced by the use of instruments as well as extra voices. Little documentation survives concerning the way in which instruments were actually used, but it is clear that motets and organa were sung by solo high-register men's voices, and that the tenor (taken from plainsong) was confined to the alto/tenor range. The likely result was thus a combined sound of male voices and higher-register instruments (the bass region not yet being used), so that the recorder may well have had an important role. The outstanding members of the school of Notre Dame in Paris (*c.*1200) were Leoninus and

Perotinus. The uniformly severe, harsh sound of this dramatic music, with its unchanging beat, is more readily understood when its dance-like character is brought out. The involvement of the musicians in the performance, and no doubt that of the listeners as well, was intense. Contemporary accounts describe ecstatic gestures and acrobatic movements on the part of the singers.

### c)  Ars Nova

The Ars Nova, which emerged in the fourteenth century, also involves the instruments of the flute family. The distinction between transverse flutes and recorders occurs early on, the two types being found together. From the start the term 'flute', unless further qualified, refers to a flute with a windway. The great composer and poet Machaut (*c*.1300–1377), for example, distinguishes between '*fleustes traversaines*' and '*fleustes, dont droit jour quand tu fleustes*'; and Deschamps, in his ballade on the death of Machaut, speaks of '*flaustes*' and '*traversaines*'. Pictorial sources show instrumental trios consisting of harp, fiddle and recorder; lute, crumhorn and harp; recorder, portative organ and harp; and lute, fiddle and recorder. In secular music, especially, combinations were particularly favoured for which the term 'split sound' has been used: thus, ideally, an ensemble would be made up of a wind instrument, a bowed instrument and a plucked instrument.

During this period the four-part motet (with the parts termed triplum, motetus, tenor and contratenor) loses its position of pre-eminence, and secular, usually three-part, refrain forms such as the rondeau, ballade and virelai make their appearance (the parts being termed cantus, tenor and contratenor). The traditional blending of vocal and instrumental parts is retained: we should imagine small solistic ensembles consisting of a few singers and a few instruments. It is also known that the upper part, or triplum, gradually shifts from male alto to boy treble. The instruments either follow the singers *colla parte* or provide a slow-moving foundation for one or two faster, elaborated solo upper parts. Machaut's ballades, for example, have a solo high male voice, which can be doubled at the octave by a recorder if desired, and between one and three instruments serving as accompaniment. If a recorder is to be used for one of the lower parts, the tenor instrument is suitable. Indeed, it is clear that a preference for lower-register recorders persisted for a considerable time. The alto/ tenor range of the tenor part, with c as its lowest note, enabled the part to be played on the tenor recorder without difficulty. It was only gradually that bass instruments proper, such as the trombone, were introduced. Not only secular compositions but motets too might be performed outside the ecclesiastical context. Even at a later date, motets by composers such as Lasso and Palestrina were treated as a form of 'sacred domestic music', often being performed purely instrumentally.

In Italy, the madrigal of the Florentine school is essentially solo vocal music but, like the caccia and ballata, it retains the mixed vocal and instrumental sound characteristic of the Ars Antiqua. The outstanding figure of the *trecento* is the blind composer Francesco Landini (d.1397), also famous as an organist. His ballatas, usually in three parts, are examples of the cantilena style,[6] with two voice parts above a supporting instrumental tenor. Whereas Machaut's music is fascinating for its bold, mordant harmony, Landini's madrigal style is notable for its gentle rhythmical subtlety.

### d) The period of the Netherlands schools

The fifteenth and sixteenth centuries are often referred to as the era of the early Netherlands schools. The growth of commerce and the crafts brought with it an ever-expanding civic influence on the arts, and this influence was particularly apparent in the Low Countries. It is the craft and manufacturing spirit that animates the strict, solidly constructed polyphonic writing of the age. For all its variety, the period has a stylistic unity. It stretches from Gilles Binchois (*c.*1400–1460) and Guillaume Dufay (*c.*1400–1474) to Johannes Ockeghem, Jakob Obrecht, Pierre de la Rue, Heinrich Isaac, Adrian Willaert, Josquin des Prez, Clemens non papa, and finally to Philipp de Monte (1521–1603) and Orlando di Lasso (1532–1594).[7] The unity of the period is founded on the technique of strict polyphony, in contrast to the Italian style with its impetus towards blended textures and homophony.

According to Wolff,[8] the Netherlands composers show features of both the Gothic and the Renaissance styles. The Renaissance group of composers includes masters such as Dufay and Binchois and, as supreme examples, Obrecht and Josquin. Gothic features are most evident in de la Rue, Agricola, Ockeghem and Gombert. Wolff offers the following defining characteristics of the two groups:

*Renaissance group*
1. Textual clarity, i.e. the music conforms to the metre of the text, and the words are set so as to be audible and comprehensible.
2. The music is a representation of the emotional content of the text.
3. Formal clarity and intelligibility, i.e. clear-cut breaks and structural subdivisions.
4. An emphasis on overall sound and auditory quality.

Hans Burgkmair, Float with musicians, from *The Triumph of Kaiser Maximilian I* (schwegel with drum, pommers, lutes, viola da braccio, viola da gamba, harp)

5. Expression is relatively restrained. (This applies only to the Renaissance period proper, not to the early baroque, i.e. after *c*.1550.)

*Gothic group*
1. Absolute music, i.e. the music is composed without reference to the text set.
2. The structure is purely musical in significance.
3. Fluid forms: an 'infinite' melodic flow without sharp breaks or subdivisions.
4. Linear voice-leading: no special concern for blended timbres, parallel movement or tonal quality.
5. Emotional expression and tension are heightened, with amassing of parts, ornaments and dissonances.

The musical forms of the period are the mass, the motet and the chanson. Examples of the first are the works of Dufay, Ockeghem and Obrecht, the masses of Josquin (influenced by the Italian high Renaissance style) and the works by Willaert, Lasso and Isaac written in the imitative style. The second category includes works by Dufay, Binchois and Brasart in the fifteenth century, the motets of Josquin and, after 1550, the emotionally charged music (musica reservata) of Philipp de Monte and Orlando di Lasso. The principal representatives of chanson writing are Binchois, Dufay and Busnois in the fifteenth century and Josquin, Clemens non papa and Isaac in the sixteenth; German *Lieder* and the dance music that evolved from the chanson are also included in this category.

All these musical forms involve the use of singers and instruments, in combination. The three-part song writing of the Dufay period (with the parts termed cantus, tenor and contratenor) still retains features of the cantilena style: the cantus, sung by female or male voices, is accompanied by instruments, with the contratenor often being realized by lute or harp. This type of setting is also found in the works of the great English master John Dunstable. The Burgundian model of '*haute et basse musique*', with its two instrumental groups, alta and bassa, gives an indication of practice with regard to instrumentation. The alta group includes the powerful instruments (trumpet, trombone, shawm, bagpipe, horn and loud percussion), while the bassa group contains the quiet instruments (recorder, lute, fiddle, viol, harp and quiet percussion). The alta instruments are thus primarily open-air ones: to be used for dance music, for example. The bassa instruments, on the other hand, are chiefly suited to intimate chamber performance. It is certainly possible for individual instruments from one group to be substituted in the other group, and the effect can be very attractive in a particular context. On grounds of tonal balance, however, there are definite advantages in keeping the two groups separated. Evidently alta and bassa would also play in alternation: pictures of the period frequently show both alta and bassa together, but spatially apart.

Singers with alta and bassa (layout based on a woodcut in *Mittelalterliches Hausbuch, c.*1475)

| Knee harp | Lute | Schwegel with hand drum |
|---|---|---|
| | BASSA | SINGERS |
| Treble pommer | Alto shawm | Tenor trombone |
| | ALTA | |

The human voice is essential to the music, much of it three-part, of the Middle Ages and early Renaissance. As we have said, this music is often expressly solistic, involving one or two voices with instrumental accompaniment. It is by no means the case that each of the parts is sung. In fact, most often the only sung part is the main part, generally the discantus or tenor. The use of contrasting timbres should be a paramount consideration: choric sound appears only in the high Renaissance and early baroque.

Vocal and instrumental music remained closely linked for a long time. Instruments could always be substituted for voices if desired, and even works in which all the parts are set to texts might be performed on instruments alone. (A late chanson example is Sweelinck's *Rimes françoises et italiennes*.)[9] Among the 'miscellaneous instruments' referred to in countless prefaces as possible substitutes for the voice, the recorder is one of the most commonly mentioned. Arnt von Aich, for example, in his *Liederbuch* of 1519, says:[10] 'In this little book will be found pretty songs, to be sung merrily by descant, alto, bass and tenor, and several for which flutes or fifes and other kinds of instrument may be used.' The many *Liederbücher* of the period offer the recorder player a wealth of fine music: the *Glogauer Liederbuch* (c.1455),[11] Oeglin (1512), Schöffer (1513),[12] von Aich (1519), Ott (1535–1544),[13] Egenolf (1535), Forster (1539–1556),[14] and Rhaw (1544). The fact that often the texts of the songs are given in full only in the tenor part-book shows that the pieces were commonly performed with a sung tenor cantus firmus and that the remaining parts were taken by instruments. A recorder can be used either to double the cantus firmus at the octave or to play the descant (when preferably a tenor recorder should be used). If the cantus firmus is sung by a soprano voice (sounding an octave higher than written), the remaining parts can be taken by a four-part ensemble of descant, treble, (tenor) and bass recorders. In Italian madrigal comedy, too, not only the musical *intermedii* but also the vocal parts were often played on instruments *colla parte*. Madrigals generally were commonly performed as mixed vocal and instrumental pieces.

On the whole, then, there were still no rigid boundaries between instrumental and vocal music. The carmina of the period around 1550, on the other hand, were pieces intended for instrumental performance from the start. Examples of carmina are found in the *Glogauer Liederbuch* and in Isaac, Senfl and Greitter;[15] they can be played either by mixed ensembles or chorically (by instruments of a single family). Early choir books and vocal instruction books often contain canons and bicinia without texts. These were intended as solmization exercises for singers, but could also be used as practice material by instrumentalists (cf. collections by Walter, Lasso, Gumpelzhaimer and Quirsfelder). Johann Walter says explicitly that his canons[16] '[...] will be useful, convenient and advantageous on all instruments of like tuning [...] and especially for ease of performance and practice by the young'.

The dance music of the fifteenth and sixteenth centuries is closely linked to the chanson writing of the Netherlands. What originated as the minstrel's improvisation on the tenor of a chanson became elaborated into the descant of a dance piece. At the same time, chansons proper were also played as instrumental dance music. The first dance music to be printed dates from about 1550 (Attaingnant, c.1520;[17] Phalèse, 1546; Susato, 1551).[18] Again, both mixed and choric settings were possible, although choric performance was increasingly gaining ground. This music contains a great range of splendid effects: different instrumental choirs can be set in contrast with one another (choirs of recorders, viols, lutes, crumhorns, and trombones with cornetts), and varying tone-colour groups can be alternated or combined in repeated passages or in different movements. Virtually all meaningful permutations are allowed; there are no fixed rules, apart from those arising from musical considerations (e.g. agile instruments to be used in fast passages, powerful instruments in solemn passages, etc.). It is advisable to try out different possibilities on different instruments, to see which ones 'work' best. The size of these ensembles is also a matter of choice: they can be very small (one player per part) or, on occasions of pageantry, very large, with each part being played by several performers (see p. 83).

As far as combinations of voices and instruments are concerned, in sacred or secular music, recorders can be used in various different ways:

a) In unison with (or doubling at the octave) one of the vocal parts, usually the cantus firmus.
b) Doubling more than one vocal part.
c) One or more of the parts played by recorders only, and not sung (e.g. for a tenor song: tenor recorder, crumhorn, sung tenor, viol).
d) All parts of a vocal choir doubled by a recorder choir.

Michael Praetorius, writing in 1619, places the recorder in the second-highest rank in the hierarchy of wind instruments, after the trumpet and trombone. By now recorders are being used in choric ensembles (or consorts) corresponding to the vocal ranges of soprano, alto, tenor and bass. According to Sebastian Virdung, two tenor recorders are used in a four-part recorder consort, and no descant recorder: in other words, the soprano part is taken by a treble recorder, tenor instruments play the alto and tenor parts, and a bass recorder plays the bass. Praetorius, too,[19] says that almost always only three types of recorder are used in four-part pieces, and he also indicates that the alto and tenor parts are to be taken by the same type of instrument. He lists the following combinations:

1. Great bass (F), bass (B flat), basset (f)
2. Bass (B flat), basset (f), tenor (c′)
3. Basset (f), tenor (c′), treble (g′)
4. Tenor (c′), treble (g′), descant (d″ or c″)

Instead of the bass recorder, a crumhorn is suggested (by Agricola), or a bass trombone or a dulcian (Praetorius). The use of the crumhorn entails certain restrictions, however, since its range is no more than a ninth or a tenth. The most suitable kind of trombone is an instrument with narrow bore, which combines excellently with the sound of the recorder and makes the bass line stand out clearly without being obtrusive. A modern bassoon would need to be played with care and restraint to avoid a clash of dynamics and timbre. The

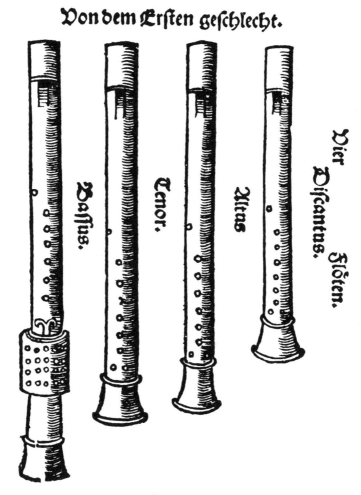

Quartet of recorders, from Agricola, *Musica instrumentalis deudsch*, 1532

dulcian, on the other hand (reproduction copies of which are now being built again), is particularly suitable for the bass part of a four-part recorder consort. Combinations of this sort, with one eight-foot instrument and three four-foot instruments, apply primarily to pieces with a genuine bass line. They work especially well if a number of instrumental choirs are involved, since the recorder bass is often weaker than its opposite numbers.

Several references in the literature indicate that the treble recorder was preferred to the descant, and the tenor to the bass, especially in mixed instrumental ensembles. Practical experience certainly bears out the advantage of using the wide-bore tenor recorder for the descant part (i.e. as an eight-foot instrument). In an ensemble where altus, tenor and bassus are taken by three viols, for instance, or by crumhorn, sung tenor and viola da gamba, the tenor recorder is easily able to hold its own in the descant part.

Whatever the way in which the recorder was being used, the 'moderation' enjoined by Praetorius was always of paramount importance. By this, Praetorius means that emphasis should be followed by relaxation of tension, and an increase in volume by a decrease. He refers to the bad habit of many orators, who 'maintain no decorum in their expression, not raising and lowering the voice as the text and *affectus* demand, but keep speaking in the same tone, without distinction. This is irksome to the ear in speech, and all the more so in singing.'[20] The instrumentalist, too, must heed this warning.

Frontispiece from Humphry Salter, *The Genteel Companion*, 1683

The inventories of princely bands and 'chapels' show the high regard in which wind instruments in general, and the recorder in particular, were held in the sixteenth century. The estate of Count Fugger (1529–1569), for example, contained 111 recorders out of a total of 507 assorted wind instruments, but merely 39 stringed instruments.[21] Music for wind was still deemed more refined than music played on strings. Strings made increasing headway in the course of the sixteenth century, and especially in the seventeenth, notably in Italian music and in music written under Italian influence.

The recorder was very highly regarded in Germany, but also in Italy, France, the Netherlands and Spain. In England, the recorder's home *par excellence*, it was held in extraordinarily high esteem. John Lydgate (*c*.1375–*c*.1450) extols it as an instrument 'ful of armonye', and laudatory references are repeatedly found in English literature. Chaucer (*c*.1340–1400), Shakespeare (1564–1616) and Milton (1608–1674), to name only three leading writers, hail its virtues, and recorder ensembles are called on to provide music in plays. Even the fact that the recorder was condemned by the Puritans only serves to show how enormously popular the instrument really was. When the Puritan John Foxe, in his *Book of Martyrs* (1563), praises the man who is made fearful by the sound of the recorder and begins to pray, he is casting the instrument as the very symbol of delight in earthly pleasures. In the eyes of Stephen Gosson, another Puritan writer, playing the recorder was actually the first step on the path to hell. This path, he said, led 'from piping to playing, from play to pleasure, from pleasure to slouth, from slouth to sleepe, from sleepe to sinne, from sinne to death, from death to the Divel'.[22]

The recorder reached the height of its popularity during the reign of Henry VIII. The king's own passion for music was characteristic of the age: he played the recorder, flute and virginal daily, and composed songs.[23] The ways in which the instrument was used were similar to those current on the Continent, although mixed instrumental ensembles, or 'broken consorts', were particularly popular. Thomas Morley, in his *Consort Lessons* of 1599, describes the following broken consort (one possibility among many): 'the Treble-Flute, the Pandora, the Citterne, the Base-Viole, the Flute and the Treble-Viole'. On the other hand, choric ensembles, or 'whole consorts', were not unknown. A large number of works were written for consorts of viols, for example (e.g. by Ferrabosco, Jenkins, Coperario, Lupo, Lawes and Locke). Much of this music is so expressly designed for strings in terms of compass and style that performance by recorder ensemble is scarcely feasible unless the music is specially adapted, but recorders can be used in these pieces as part of a broken consort of different instruments.

# Stylistic questions in the fourteenth, fifteenth and sixteenth centuries

### a) Articulation

Historically speaking, it is clear that instrumental articulation developed out of the articulation used in singing and hence, indirectly, out of the articulation of speech.

In the music of the Middle Ages and the Renaissance, which is predominantly vocal, it is natural and obvious that instrumental articulation should have been modelled on the articulation of the vocal parts. When one performs the richly structured and rhythmically complex works of the school of Notre Dame, say, it is clear that there must be very careful gradations of articulation. Even though this music is notated without articulatory markings, the instrumentalist must mirror the way in which the text is enunciated and subdivided. Following the sung text with ear and eye is therefore essential.

Heavy contrasts of articulation should generally be avoided, depending on the size of the space used for performance and the scale of instrumental forces involved. It should be remembered that the taste for highly varied modes of articulation did not really develop until the seventeenth and eighteenth centuries, in parallel with the conscious use of shadings in tempo and dynamics. According to Keller,[24] the legato singing style – which corresponds to tongued legato (portato) on the recorder – was 'the sole and undisputed expression of the melodic line and was the preserve of sacred music from the start. The "legato style", as far as both composition and performance are concerned, was the paradigmatic church style.' Detached playing, on the other hand, belonged to purely instrumental music, notably to dance music. Diruta[25] recommends this type of articulation 'in order to give more grace to the dances'. It can be used in all pieces in which rhythm takes precedence over the melodic line and in which rapid or complex rhythmic patterns need to be clearly brought out. It is also necessary in large resonant places.

The emergence of a specifically instrumental style of contrastive articulation is part and parcel of the rise of purely instrumental forms. The recorder is an instrument that responds swiftly and sensitively to interruptions of the air-stream produced by movements of the tongue, and instruction books on the flute family (which appear comparatively early) go into these questions very thoroughly. In particular, articulation by means of specific 'lingue', or syllables, is taught in numerous works on wind playing. The broad rule in the sixteenth and seventeenth centuries is that large note-values are emphasized by incisive articulation and small note-values are made smooth and supple by soft articulation. In later centuries these principles are largely reversed.

Sylvestro Ganassi[26] was the first writer to set out a syllabic system of articulation specifically relevant to the recorder. He gives three *lingue principali*:

> *le re*
> *te re* (also *de re*)
> *te che*

The same syllables are regularly found in later pedagogic works. Martin Agricola[27] gives fewer variants. He recommends *de* as the main form of tonguing, while for *semiminima* he suggests either the same syllable or *diri*, which is also given for *fusa*. He prescribes '*Flitterzunge*' (*tellellellellell*) for rapid coloration. As in Ganassi, the first syllable of a pair of syllables is stressed. This is made clear by the stress in Agricola's rhyme:

> *Willtu das dein pfeiffen besteh*
> *Lern wol das diridiride*

(If you wish your piping to succeed, be sure to learn the *diridiride*)

Hieronymus Cardanus[28] also uses the three main forms of articulation given above. In Philibert Jambe de Fer[29] we read of the need for good tonguing technique and of a method of playing in which each note is tongued. He also gives the delightful advice: 'If you enjoy your playing, be sure not to let your tongue get mouldy – in other words, drink frequently.' Mersenne, too,[30] gives the general rule that each note should be articulated, but he also refers to two-note slurs (♩♩ ♩♩), as does Fantini.[31] Bismantova also recognizes this
<sub>ta a ta a</sub>
slurred articulation, and gives an example of '*lingua* [...] *legata*':

de,     de, a,  de, a, de, a, de

Often the cornett and recorder are covered in the same instruction book, but only occasionally does an author refer expressly to the difference in incisiveness of attack on the two instruments. According to Bismantova, for example, the *te* of the cornett becomes *de* on the recorder.[32] With careful checking by ear, and by slightly softening the onset consonants, it is possible to transfer directly many of the instructions on articulation for the cornett on to the recorder.

Girolamo dalla Casa,[33] Richardo Rogniono[34] and Francesco Rognoni Taegio[35] are basically in accord with Ganassi and Cardanus as far as the rules of articulation are concerned.

Simple tonguing

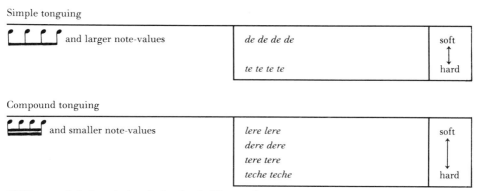

| ♪♪♪♪ and larger note-values | de de de de | soft ↕ hard |
| | te te te te | |

Compound tonguing

| ♪♪♪♪ and smaller note-values | lere lere | soft ↑ ↓ hard |
| | dere dere | |
| | tere tere | |
| | teche teche | |

NB The sound *che*, in *teche*, is articulated as *ke*. The sound *re*, in *lere* etc., is not rolled but is produced almost like a *de* (with the tongue tip).

For Ganassi the articulation *teche* sounds '*crudo ed aspro*'; for Rognoni it even has a '*barbara natura*'. Practical trials will show, however, that very different musical results follow depending how hard or softly the initial consonants *t* and *k* are articulated. Very rapid festoons of notes, as found in diminutions to madrigals, for instance,[36] can be articulated smoothly using soft 'double-tonguing' (approximately *dege*). This may also be the meaning of the softer variant *dacha* mentioned by Ganassi. Ganassi gives several further unusual sets of syllables: *cha, che, chi, cho, chu*, and *tar, ter, tir, tor, tur*, and even *lar, ler, lir, lor, lur*. It is possible, however, that these are not articulations actually used in playing but are meant to be used as tongue exercises.

A satisfactory system of 'pronunciation' requires using simple and/or compound tonguings in combination. There are certain general principles:

a) The first note in a note-group should receive emphasis:

| te | re | le | re | le | and | de | re | le | re | le |

b) Changes in the interval pattern of a melody should be brought out by changes of syllable:

de re le re le de de

c) The target note of a phrase also often needs a clear attack:

te re le re le re te

Rognoni gives a particularly illuminating example of an imaginative use of different syllables, involving departures from the strict rules:

(Syllables which would conform to the standard rules are given in parentheses.)

The effect produced by the soft articulation *lere* is regularly referred to as '*dolce*' and held to be of fundamental importance. The tongue is directed slightly upwards against the roof of the mouth ('*lingua riversa*'), which produces the smoothness and fluency characteristic of this form of articulation. By contrast, Rognoni refers to *te* (or *de*) and *tere* (or *dere*) as '*lingua diritta*'. Here the tongue is extended  straight ahead (on the first syllable in the case of the syllable pairs) and the tonguing action is a forward movement (*diritta*).

It seems likely that a new type of articulatory practice developed during the first half of the seventeenth century, particularly in northern Europe. This may be the basis for Vicenzo's comment in 1628[37] that the German style and artistry on the recorder was only rarely to be found in Italy. Bismantova (1677), at any rate, still adheres fully to the north-Italian tradition:

<table>
<tr><td>te   te   re   te</td><td>te   re   te   te</td><td>re   le   re   te   re   le   re   te</td><td>re   te.</td></tr>
</table>

Slurred playing (true legato) is very much the exception in sixteenth-century music. According to Agricola, if a player is not to sound 'like the peasants', all notes should be tongued. Dalla Casa plainly prefers a tongued attack (*batter la lingua*) to playing with *lingua morta*, maintaining that unarticulated playing is the resort of those who have not mastered *lingua riversa*. Nevertheless, Ganassi describes 'another way of making the sound, which employs no syllables whatever and is known as *lingua di testa*. Here the breath is formed by the lips and flows out between them.'[38] This account presumably refers to an unarticulated legato. Unfortunately, however, the circumstances under which it is to be used are not stated.

The emergence of a solistic style after 1600 leads to a steady increase in the number of references to legato playing, Indeed, legato on stringed instruments is acknowledged earlier (cf. Ortiz,[39] Rogniono and Cerreto),[40] though primarily for purposes of improving bowing technque and only rarely as an expressive device. The new virtuoso violin literature, however, reveals other circumstances under which slurs can be deliberately introduced. They are used to facilitate the playing of particularly rapid figures and ornamental flourishes, for example, and also to give emphasis to important notes or to lessen emphasis on unimportant ones (e.g. harmony notes versus passing notes). Instruction books for wind instruments are scarce in this period, but analogous references can be found, as mentioned earlier, in Mersenne (1636) and Fantini (1638).

From now onward, legato is an expressive device to be used at the discretion of the musician. This continues to be the case during the high baroque and, with some qualifications, in the classical era. The use of legato to make rapid playing as smooth as possible or to create an extreme *espressivo* comes only later.


### b) Ornamentation

Improvisations which depart from the original notes of a piece, while remaining based on them, have always been a part of musical performance. Instrumental and vocal ornamentation, by the single musician and by ensembles, can be traced back to the earliest stages of recorded musical history. Using a combination of imagination and research, and with the aid of surviving examples and theoretical accounts of ornamentation, we are in a position today to build up a better picture of the original sound-quality and expressive character of early music, and to bring it to life again in our own age.

Two separate categories of ornamentation, or diminution, appear very early on, though the boundary between them is not a precise one, especially in medieval and Renaissance music. The first category is ornamentation used at significant points in the architecture or content of a composition. This 'foregrounding' effect is created by an 'increase in tonal mass', i.e. by the break-up of larger note-values into a number of smaller ones,[41] involving appoggiaturas as well as the particular note being emphasized. The other type of ornamentation is melodic differentiation, produced by alternation of the melodic shape of one of the parts, usually the upper. Individual notes are freely embellished and intervals are filled in.

Trill-like embellishments of a note with its neighbouring whole-tone or semitone second (*flores longae, aperti, subiti*) and appoggiaturas and turns (*reverberationes*) are mentioned in thirteenth-century sources.[42] Lengthy melismas over the closing cadence in fourteenth-century music, emphasizing a passage of structural importance, belong to the first category of *diminutio*, while coloration (including coloration of the cantus firmus) by means of 'beautiful ascending and descending passages'[43] can be assigned to the second category. Tunstede (in 1351) states the important principle that *diminutio* should under no circumstances obscure or impede the discantus. Furthermore, 'in accordance with the edicts of the Curia, as well as the custom of the French *déchanteurs* and of all singers of music, the tenor [should] properly be sung unaltered'.[44] The minstrels' use of free diminutions and improvised organa (accompaniments, usually in bourdon fifths) also comes under this second heading.

The use of *diminutio* naturally entails a new emphasis on solo performance, as regards both voices and instruments. The art of ornamentation thus evolves as part and parcel of the emergence of solo parts from within the ensemble, although it is clear that instrumental music always follows in the footsteps of vocal music, the dependence of instrumental music on speech and song being finally broken only in the early baroque period. The relationship between vocal and instrumental music is clearly the basis for the improvisatory character of instrumental music (which at first is scarcely ever notated) and hence for instrumental *diminutio*.[45] Providing unaccompanied improvisations on a cantus firmus is a very rich field for recorder players.

The combination of main parts proceeding in long notes and upper parts characterized by rich ornamentation, so common in fifteenth-century composition, signals the transition between polyphony, now in gradual decline, and the newly emergent homophonic style. The slow-moving part increasingly comes to serve as the foundation of the harmonic structure and is hence usually left unornamented. Sixteenth-century theoretical writings on *diminutio* attempt to codify improvisation practice, which until then had been left to the freedom of the performer. In most cases the new rules deal with vocal and instrumental ornamentation simultaneously. Ganassi (1535), for example, says that his book on the recorder will also be 'suitable for all other wind and stringed instruments, and for singers'. Many writers provide information or ornamentation in this period, including Johannes Tinctoris (*c*.1487), Martin Agricola (1528/1545), Diego Ortiz (1553), Adrian Petit-Coclicus (1552), Hermann Finck (1556), Giovanni Luca Conforto (1693) and Thomas Morley (1597).[46]

The term 'vibrato' in this period denotes all forms of ornamentation which involve either a fluctuation between two pitches or the repetition (as smooth as possible) of a single pitch. The frequency and amplitude of the vibrato can be very varied.[47] With instruments of the flute family we must also distinguish between two different types of vibrato: finger vibrato and breath vibrato.

The chief method of producing finger vibrato is to cover or half-cover the finger-hole (or the next but one finger-hole) below the fingering for the note. This gives a vibrato which flattens the main pitch. Ganassi[48] and Cardanus[49] also describe finger vibrati (*tremoli*) which produce a trill-like sharpening of the main note. Finger vibrato can also be played '*V*[*ivace*]' or '*S*[*uave*]': this distinction may denote louder and softer versions, with appropriate fingerings. Blanckenburgh (1654) speaks of at least one, and often several, *Trammelante* for each note, and English 'Companions'[50] follow suit. Cardanus describes the resulting vibrations as ranging from a quarter-tone to a major third.

The first edition of Agricola's *Musica instrumentalis deudsch* of 1528 contains the famous lines:

*Auch wiltu haben den grund und boden*
*So lern pfeiffen mit zitterndem odem*
*Denn es den gesang gantz sere zyret*
*Auff allen pfeiffen wie man hofiret*

(And if you desire a true foundation, learn to pipe with trembling breath. For singing is greatly adorned when it is paid court by all the pipes)

This is a clear reference to a breath vibrato. The vibrato, evidently a rapid one, is actually seen as the foundation of recorder playing. Elsewhere Agricola again insists explicitly that 'you blow with trembling breath'. Comparisons with 'trembling' in singing and on the *Polische Geige* and the organ underline further the importance of this expressive device in making the melody sing 'more sweetly'.[51] Ganassi says that the string player's bowing hand and fingering hand may 'tremble', but does not describe the occasions when this form of ornamentation is appropriate. Cardanus, who is plainly influenced by Ganassi on many points of detail, mentions a '*vox tremula*'[52] produced by movements of breath and fingers, though unfortunately he also omits to explain the part played by breathing. Seventeenth-century instruction books indicate that a gently articulated note-repetition vibrato was recognized on both stringed and wind instruments:

(Rognoni)

It is likely that this form of ornamentation derived from the '*ribattuta di gola*', a species of laryngeal vibrato used in singing. Whether this 'beating with the throat' was copied on wind instruments by an adaptation of a singer's throat technique, or by means of a close succession of tongue movements (tongued legato), is not known for certain. Indeed, originally both methods may have been used.

It is assumed that the term '*trillo*' refers to this sort of note-repetition, produced in one of these two ways. '*Tremolo*', on the other hand, may denote 'an alternating swell and decrease in the sound'.[53] When Rognoni, therefore, says that the *trillo* is a *ribattuta di gola*, it is plausible to assume that the *tremolo* is produced by some other means.

The speeds of these two types of vibrato are never given by category, and indeed are rarely specified at all. Nevertheless, the term 'trembling' would appear to indicate a rapid vibratory process. Cardanus even mentions the trembling of a sword set in vibration. On the other hand, one reason why Praetorius[54] commends the *Geigenwerk* or clavicymbal-violin is that it can be used to play music 'with a free hand, slowly or fast, shaking and trembling'.

Praetorius also regards the ability of the singing voice to tremble and shake[55] as a gift of God or nature: a 'delightful trembling and shaking of the voice [...] with especial moderation' is one of the three essential characteristics of good singing. By 'moderation', as we have noted, Praetorius means the raising and lowering of the voice, in the sense of an increase and reduction of the sound produced.[56] In his view it is a shortcoming of keyboard instruments that they are unable to provide such dynamic shadings. For Praetorius, in other words, vibrato entails a variation in dynamic level – a link which clearly persists through all periods of musical history. For him, as for other writers, vibrato is obviously a means of creating a sweeter and more attractive sound. Ganassi, incidentally, recommends that in sad music the string player play with a trembling movement in both his bowing arm and the fingers of the hand on the finger-board.[57] Antegnati, finally, advises the use of the organ tremulant (which he refers to as *voce umana* or *Fiffaro*) only if no diminutions are played. Players who perform ornamented pieces using the tremulant are guilty of bad taste, '*perché rende confusione*'. He likewise warns against the distortions of intonation which occur when a part with vibrato is coupled with one without.[58]

A survey of the sources, then, shows that vibrato in the sixteenth and seventeenth centuries had a great variety of uses as an expressive ornamental device. Recorder players can pick up all sorts of playing suggestions from accounts originally intended for other instruments. The guiding rule, apart from a player's own taste and judgement, should be to imitate the human voice.

All early sets of examples illustrate the procedures of breaking up longer melodic notes into shorter ones and filling in leaps between notes. Particular embellishments which readily suggested themselves at standard points in a piece (e.g. at the final cadence) eventually evolved into set ornaments, entitled *groppo, tremolo, trillo, ribattuta, accento, cascata, tirata* and so on. These ornaments belong to the first of our two categories, ornaments used to create emphasis.

Free diminutions of individual parts (which fall within the second category, melodic variation) are refined, taking the form of virtuoso runs and embellishments, often for the purpose of conveying emotional effects. The bass is usually left unaltered.

The various possible types of ornamentation may be classified as follows:

i.   Ornamentation of structurally important points in the music (*groppo, trillo*, etc.).

ii. Free ornamentation, especially of larger note-values (sparing at the beginning of a piece, increasing at mid-point and fullest at the end).

iii. The variation principle: diminutions of a melody when it is repeated.

iv. Alternating ornamentation of different voices/parts in a composition.

Ornamentation should not be overdone. Finck compares the breaking-up of a vocal line to the shredding of a rag by young dogs, and the literature contains repeated warnings against faulty progressions caused by poor ornamentation. Ortiz advises those learning the art of ornamentation to begin by writing ornaments out in full and then to develop the technique of improvisation gradually. Impromptu instrumental ornamentation is an essential feature of the music of the period, and yet some of Ganassi's model examples, for instance, show that the basic types of ornament keep cropping up.

The overall trend within the period is as follows:

i.   Ornamentation is quite free and unrestricted.

ii.  Particular types of diminution formula are used *ad libitum*.

iii. Distinct, non-interchangeable ornaments are established, and are indicated by fixed symbols.

According to Ortiz, writing in the sixteenth century – about half-way through this process of evolution – the player must 'weigh up his own dexterity and choose those variations which seem to him best in the light of it. However good the variation, if the hand cannot perform it, it cannot succeed.'[59] Both theoretical considerations and the motoric aspects of improvisation executed for pleasure's sake are therefore relevant. Indeed, the two can easily come into conflict. Even Ortiz, who clearly tends to adhere to a theorist's point of view, advises that in certain cases the player should[60] 'be guided roughly by his ear, without knowing for certain what he is playing'. In other words, knowledge of the basic rules of good composition, an attentive ear and, at the same time, a readiness to give free yet guided rein to the natural instinct for improvisation are all vital for authentic stylistically faithful *diminutio*.

*Free ornamentation*

Filling-in of intervals and embellishment of parts of a melody

Konrad Paumann (1450)

Sylvestro Ganassi (1535)

Diego Ortiz (1535)
(Descant variation of *O felici occhi miei*)

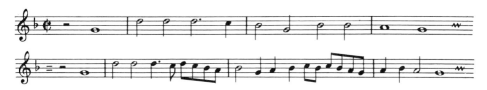

Adrian Petit-Coclicus (1552)
(*Fuga quatuor vocum ex una*)

1st entry          2nd entry          3rd entry          4th entry

*Elegans*

## Cadences

Sylvestro Ganassi (1535)

(This example contains diminution formulae which gradually evolve into set ornaments: 1 *groppo*; 2 *tremuletto*; 3 *tremulo*; 4 mordent)

Lodovico Zacconi (1592)

Giovanni Bassano (1598)

## Set ornaments

Trill
Girolamo Diruta (1598)

Mordent
Tomas a Santa Maria (1565)

Turn
Tomas a Santa Maria (1565)

(The *redoble* preceding a semibreve is played very quickly)

Appoggiatura
Girolamo Diruta (1598)

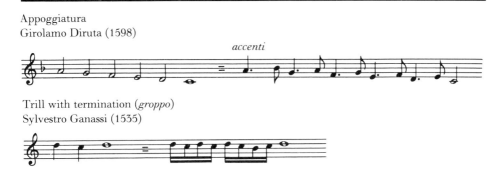

accenti

Trill with termination (*groppo*)
Sylvestro Ganassi (1535)

### c) Notation

Various improvements on the rough notation of melody by the neumes were made in the course of the Middle Ages. Staves were introduced to determine pitch. Guido of Arezzo (*c*.980–1050) used stave lines in different colours, writing only a single note in the spaces between them. Square notation came in during the twelfth century as an addition to neumes written on the stave lines. The same period saw the switch to mensural notation, in which rhythmic and metrical relationships between notes are indicated.

| | | | | |
|---|---|---|---|---|
| ◤ | *maxima* | | ↓ | *minima* |
| ◤ | *longa* | | ♪ [♮] | *semiminima* |
| ◤ | *brevis* | | ♪ [♮] | *fusa* |
| ◆ | *semibrevis* | | ♪ [♮] | *semifusa* |

Important notational changes took place at the time of the Ars Nova of the fourteenth century. The signs for notes were now as follows (and were not supplanted till about 1600, by the signs in use today):

| | | | | |
|---|---|---|---|---|
| ⊐ | *maxima* | | ↑ | *minima* |
| ⊐ | *longa* | | ↑ | *semiminima* |
| ⊟ | *brevis* | | ♭ | *fusa* |
| ◇ | *semibrevis* | | ♭ | *semifusa* |

### d) Tempo

Contemporary sources giving details on questions of tempo in medieval music are scarce, and there are few modern studies dealing with these problems either. Heinrich Besseler and Willi Apel[61] provide the most helpful accounts. The tempi suggested by Dart[62] would certainly not have applied universally, but they may be taken as a useful guide:

| c.1200 | longa | = | 80MM |
|---|---|---|---|
| c.1250 | brevis | = | 120MM |
| c.1280 | brevis | = | 80MM |
| c.1320 | semibrevis | = | 120MM |
| c.1350 | semibrevis | = | 80MM |
| c.1400–1500 | semibrevis | = | 50MM (with time signature O or C) |
| | semibrevis | = | 100MM (with time signature Ȼ or ¢ ) |
| | semibrevis | = | 70MM (with time signature C 3/2) |
| | semibrevis | = | 40MM (with time signature C 3 or ¢ 3/2) |

Tempo in mensural music has not yet acquired the status of an independent compositional factor. The term 'tempus' is defined in terms of relative note-values: the system of note-values is viewed as a totality, and time is measured in terms of the basic value of the notes in a given case. The 'integer valor notarum' is a temporal unit which is perceived as normal, and all smaller note-values are determined by reference to it. Tempo, in other words, may be modified on the basis of differing weightings of the note-values.

The duration of the *integer valor* varies from piece to piece: it is governed by the density of the compositional texture and the rhythmic, melodic and sound structure. Gafurius (1496)[63] gives an approximate specification, citing the pulse-rate of a person breathing normally. According to Buchner (c.1550),[64] the criterion is the time elapsing 'between two strides of a man walking at a moderate pace'. A composition notated in *longae* has a leisurely tempo; one in *fusae* is faster. The terms given in Vicentino (1555)[65] relate, not to the speed of the beat in a composition, but to its note-values. He gives the following classification:

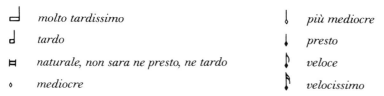

Here the value 'mediocre' is the *integer valor*. The other values are subdivisions or expansions of this mean value. If smaller note-values are in the majority, defining the character of a composition, then the *integer valor* itself shifts accordingly. The very notational appearance of a piece is thus an expression of its tempo.

Almost all Renaissance authors are agreed that the tempo of a composition must not fluctuate, even when diminutions are being played. An even beat would be given by one of the musicians in the group acting as leader. There were no bar-lines in the modern sense, so that there was no conception of a regularly emphasized 'One' or downbeat. Generally speaking, there is no upbeat in the music of the period either: trochaic articulation (*dére* etc.) thus effectively comes about of its own accord. Substantial changes of tempo were not customary: tempo was closely regulated by note-values and proportional signs.

Only towards 1600 do we begin to find occasional references to tempo modifications in the literature, with a new style of performance now in the offing. (Caccini's collection, published in 1601, is indeed called *Le nuove musiche*.) The monodic style no longer calls for formality and restraint. Its aim is the direct expression of human psychological states by the performer and the production of corresponding states within the listener. The idea of the upbeat begins to take hold, and this is reflected in the gradual emergence of iambic articulation (*turú, dirí* etc.). Stress gradually becomes more regular, and recurring rhythmical shapes appear. Much of the expressiveness in the new music now comes from exercising the freedom of 'going against the beat'. It is important for the player to identify those pieces or sections of pieces where this is the case and to handle them accordingly. Music of this transitional period involving the recorder includes works by Frescobaldi, Castello, Fontana, Selma and Montalbano, among others.[66]

*e) Suggestions for instrumentation*

Guillaume de Machaut

*Messe de Nostre Dame*[67]

i) *Gloria*

| Vocal: | | Instrumental: | |
|---|---|---|---|
| | Triplum | | Treble recorder 4′ + pommer 8′ |
| | Motetus | | Regal 4′ + fiddle 8′ |
| | Tenor | | Pommer |
| | Contratenor | | Trombone |

Singers and instruments *colla parte*; bars 93–7, *a capella*; bars 98–105, 4′ instruments silent; bars 106–31, *tutti*.

ii) *Sanctus*

| Vocal: | | Instrumental: | |
|---|---|---|---|
| | Triplum | | Pommer |
| | Motetus | | Fiddle + regal |
| | Tenor | | Trombone |
| | (Contratenor instrumental) | | Pommer |

Bars 1–15, singers and instruments as above; bars 16–63, triplum with tenor recorder instead of pommer; bars 64–94, triplum with tenor recorder + pommer.

### Glogauer Liederbuch

i)   Tenor song, 'Ich bins erfreut', 4 parts

| | |
|---|---|
| Descant | Tenor recorder |
| Contratenor alto | Treble viol or fiddle |
| Tenor | Sung by tenor, with lute |
| Contratenor bassus | Dulcian or bass crumhorn |

ii)   Tenor song, 'Mein gmüth das wüth', 3 parts

| | |
|---|---|
| Descant | Recorder 4' + cornett 8' |
| Tenor | Sung by tenor, with lute 8' |
| Contratenor | Treble viol 4' + tenor viol 8' |

iii)   Instrumental piece, 'Der pfauen schwanz', 4 parts

Recorder 4'
Tenor gamba
Crumhorn
Lute

iv)   Instrumental piece, 'Die katzenpfote', 3 parts

Treble recorder
Tenor recorder
Lute

If necessary, the treble pommer can be replaced by an oboe and the tenor pommer by a bassoon (or a cor anglais, depending on the compass). Instead of the fiddle, a violin or treble viol can be used, while the dulcian can be replaced by a bassoon. The timbre of the cornett is unique, but some other melodic instrument must be used if a cornett is not available. Performance on authentic instruments, however, is undoubtedly preferable.

## The recorder between 1600 and 1750

### a) Early baroque

Two features, more than any other, characterize the music of the Renaissance: the development of polyphony, and the dominance of music set to texts. In the second half of the sixteenth century, however, early baroque

features start to emerge. There is a new feeling for sound quality, and specialized instrumental technique begins to develop. Nevertheless, the Renaissance
and baroque styles co-exist and overlap at first, and it is only gradually that a
clear division between text-based and purely instrumental music is established.

Late sixteenth-century musical life was sustained by the bands and
'chapels' of the princely courts, and by civic musicians. The court ensembles, of
which the Bavarian Hofkapelle under Orlando di Lasso (c.1570) is a good
example, included recorder players:

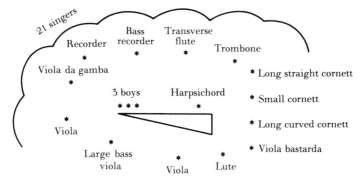

The layout is based on the picture by Hans Mielich (1570) in the autograph of Lasso's
*Penitential Psalms* (arrangement following Schering, *op. cit.*, p. 66). Schering describes the
bass recorder as a pommer, but the shape and various other features of the instrument
(the labium and the S-shaped crook) indicate the bass member of the recorder family.

Music was also taken for granted as a feature of burgher life. It was an
integral part of major events and the daily round alike, being used at weddings,
funerals and processions, in church and at the feast table, on high days and
holidays. Recorders are often mentioned among the instruments played. The
Basle physician Felix Platter (1536–1614), for example, assembled a collection
of sixty-one instruments, and ten of these – the largest single category – were
recorders.

Since the connection between voices and instruments remained very
close, it was natural that a singing-like style of recorder playing should con-
tinue, especially in works for combined vocal and instrumental forces. Contemporary instruction books on recorder playing invariably hold up singing as
a model, and the fact that the recorder can be played in a singing style is
regularly cited as one of its special advantages. The term 'singing', however,
should not be taken to mean a homogeneous, uniformly smooth form of
playing, as some twentieth-century writers have assumed. Just as singers must
aim for liveliness and contrast – they are urged by Gioseffo Zarlino (1517–
1590), for example, not to elide adjacent consonants – so wind players are told

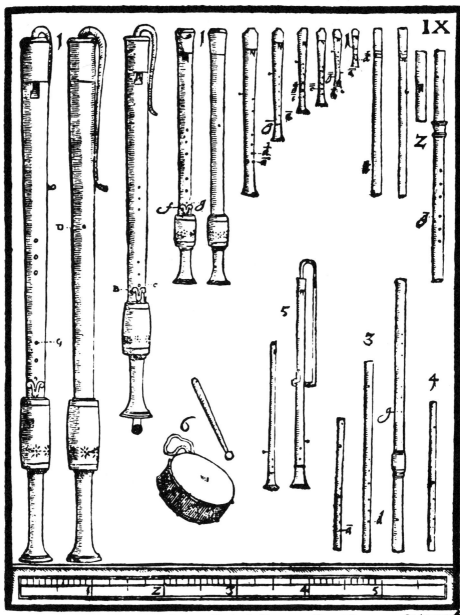

Praetorius, *Syntagma musicum*, II, 1619–1620, Plate IX

to make clarity and intelligibility their overriding goal. In singing, enunciation and interpretation of the words must be done with the utmost care, and the instrumentalist must pay similar heed to the form and meaning of the music he is playing. This is especially true of music written for voices and instruments in combination, where the instrumentalist must follow the text and mirror the rises and falls of the speech melody.

Michael Praetorius[68] describes a recorder '*Accort*' or consort consisting of eight recorders ranked as follows: *klein Flötlein* (sopranino) in $g''$, descant recorder in $d''$, descant recorder in $c''$, treble recorder in $g'$, tenor recorder in $c'$, basset recorder in f, bass recorder in B flat, and great bass recorder in F. Mersenne[69] also refers to recorders of these types, dividing them into a four-foot choir and an eight-foot choir: the first group comprises a treble, two tenors and a basset, the second a basset, two basses and a great bass. The two groups of instruments can also be combined. In organ building the term 'foot' refers to the dimensions of the open organ pipes, and this terminology is also extended to other instruments. An eight-foot organ pipe gives the note C, a four-foot pipe gives a note an octave higher (c), and a sixteen-foot pipe gives a note an octave lower ($C_1$). Modern recorders can be combined in eight-foot and four-foot choirs, e.g. as follows:

Eight-foot choir
(treble, treble, tenor
[or treble], bass
[or tenor])

Four-foot choir
(descant [or sopranino],
descant, treble, tenor
[or treble])

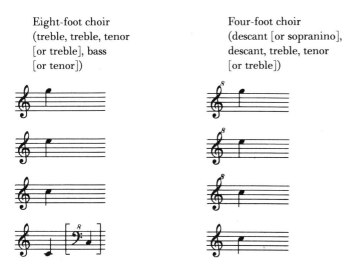

Performances with an eight-foot consort are not common today, but they produce a splendid sound and are much to be recommended. The contrastive effect produced by the use of two choirs, a four-foot and an eight-foot, can also be very fine. Praetorius urged recorder makers to build fourth-pitched instruments corresponding to each of the existing types, in order to allow all keys to be reached comfortably. Within the recorder family that expanded along these

lines, the instruments in f, c′, f′ and c″ then proved themselves the most versatile. A consort consisting of these four instruments is the one primarily found today. The treble instrument, in turn, emerged to become a solo instrument of the high baroque.

Around 1600, the desire for splendour and brilliance of sound led to the creation, in suitably large performance spaces, of special contrastive effects involving two or more instrumental and/or vocal choirs. References to this polychoral style date from as early as 1475, and Josquin des Prez and Clemens non papa used the technique. The instrumental blocs may either be mixed or may consist of single instrumental families. Here are a few examples of ceremonial ensembles of this sort, taken from documents of the court of the Medici in Florence:[70]

i) Open-air music

1539 (marriage of Cosimo I and Leonora of Toledo)
8-part motet: 24 singers + 4 cornetts and 4 trombones

ii) Chamber music

1565 (marriage of Prince Francesco and Johanna of Austria)

| | |
|---|---|
| 1. 8-part madrigal ('Venus') | 8 singers + 2 harpsichords (offstage), 4 bass viols, 1 cornett, 1 trombone, 2 recorders |
| 2. 5-part madrigal ('Love') | 5 singers + 2 harpsichords (offstage), 1 archlute, 1 improvising treble viol and 1 improvising bass viol, 4 recorders, 1 improvising recorder |
| 3. 4-part madrigal ('Zephyrus and Music') | 4 singers + 1 viol and 1 lyrone (onstage), 3 harpsichords, 1 archlute, 1 treble viol, 1 treble recorder, 1 tenor recorder, 1 improvising cornett (offstage) |
| 4. 6-part madrigal ('The Magician') | 8 singers (descant and bass doubled) + 6 crumhorns and 1 cornett |
| 5. 6-part madrigal ('Discord') | 12 singers + 2 trombones, 1 dulcian, 2 cornetts, 1 tenor cornett, 2 drums |
| 6. 5-part madrigal ('Psyche') | 1 soprano + 4 viols, 1 lyrone and 4 trombones (offstage) |

Facing page: Master of the Glorification of Mary (c.1500), *The Glorification of Mary* (detail)

7. 4-part madrigal          'Very loud and joyful': 4 singers per part
   ('Olympus')              +2 cornetts, 2 trombones, 1 dulcian,
                            1 treble crumhorn, 1 treble rebec,
                            2 lutes


   iii)  Church music

1569    40-part motet by Striggio: two vocal choirs of 8 voices each + 8 trombones, 8 viols, 8 recorders, 1 bass lute, 1 harpsichord


Madrigals were not performed simply as the composer had notated them. One or more of the parts would be ornamented, and entire additional contrapuntal parts might be improvised.

Recorders are used in sacred polychoral works either on their own or, for preference, with other wind instruments as part of the *Capellchor* (main choir or *cappella*). The smaller, contrasting *coro favorito* often provides a literal repetition of the music of the first choir: Heinrich Schütz labels the second choir in his Psalm 100[71] 'Echo'. The conventions of the period permit this echo choir to be both vocal and instrumental, though care must be taken that the singers sing the complete text, with no words omitted.[72] It is also feasible in some polychoral works for the *coro favorito* alone to be sung, the *capella* choir (or choirs) being realized instrumentally.[73] Instrumental realization of individual vocal parts is also mentioned as a possibility by various authors (e.g. Praetorius and Schütz), and it is even possible for merely one of the middle-range or lower vocal parts, say, to be sung while the others are played on instruments.

An idea of the fluid relationship between voices and instruments is given by the settings which Johann Hermann Schein lists for his *Waldliederlein*:[74]

   i)    All parts (2 sopranos and 1 bass) sung or played on keyboard (intabulated)
   ii)   The two soprano parts performed by two tenors, with bass
   iii)  Sung by soprano, tenor and bass
   iv)   Soprano parts sung; bass part played by trombone, bassoon or violin
   v)    First soprano sung; second soprano played by violin or recorder; bass part played by one of the bass instruments (cf. (iv) above)
   vi)   First soprano and thorough-bass only; second soprano may be omitted
   vii)  Recorder or violin may play an 'additional part, which even a poor musician will easily be able to devise'(!)

Paul Peuerl's instructions regarding the performance of his dance pieces (1625)[75] are similar in character, although the settings are purely instrumental.

To a large degree, the church choral music of the Reformation also involved instruments, especially wind. Wind instruments could reinforce or be substituted for individual vocal parts, or could double or replace all of the choral parts, along the lines just described. This kind of performance of church choral music[76] is coming back into use today, and indeed has inspired modern composers to write works in which the choice of voices and instruments is flexible in the same way.

It was the Venetian composers, notably Willaert, Gabrieli and Monteverdi, who began to make a clearer separation between vocal and instrumental music. Instrumental accompaniments and purely instrumental writing both became more independent. Instruments gradually ceased merely to double the voices and were given obbligato passages or allotted the task of introducing, interrupting or rounding off the sung music. Praetorius is very informative about this new instrumental music,[77] which he encountered in Gabrieli, Leone Leoni, Steffano Bernardi and Monteverdi. Generally, an introductory piece is termed '*sinfonia*', while an interlude is termed '*ritornello*' or '*intermedium*'.[78] Sinfonias were short, pithy pieces of writing 'a sweet *harmonia*, which is played in 4, 5 or 6 parts on instruments of one kind or of all kinds, without the aid of the singers, at the beginning of the concerto and the sung music'. Instead of a sinfonia, dances might be played, or madrigals performed on instruments. Similarly, dances or canzonettas (originally sung) might take the place of a specially written ritornello. At first such pieces too were rarely more than between twelve and twenty bars long, and only gradually became more substantial.

In the same period the sonata and canzona emerge as larger forms for instrumental ensemble.[79] Praetorius explains the difference between the two as follows:[80] 'In my judgement, however, the difference is that the sonatas are composed with solemnity and splendour, like motets, whereas the canzonas move in lively, cheerful and rapid fashion with many black notes.' Gabrieli's *Canzoni per sonar* (1615) and Frescobaldi's canzonas (1628) *per ogni sorti d'istromenti* [...] are examples of the second type of piece and sound excellent on recorders. As an example of the sonata, the Sonatella for five recorders and basso continuo by Antonio Bertali (1605–1669)[81] certainly has 'solemnity and splendour' and is well suited for insertion into larger secular or sacred works as an introductory or interlude piece.

The north Italian canzona, sinfonia and sonata, however, are also the first examples of solo instrumental music with thorough-bass. Pieces by Frescobaldi, Castello and others exemplify the new instrumental style after 1600, and in 1713 Johann Mattheson still refers to the alternation between *Allegro* and *Adagio* characteristic of this music. These latter terms themselves represent a combination of old and new, serving as they do both to confirm and supplement the indications of formal structure given by note-values and *tactus* directions.

Early examples of unaccompanied music for recorder are ricercars by Giovanni Bassano (1585)[82] and Aurelio Virgiliano (late sixteenth century).[83] Both composers distinguish between *flauto* and *traversa*. In places these ricercars call for a highly virtuoso technique. Their musical value is variable: some of the works are attractive, satisfying examples of the genre, while others are more in the nature of technical exercises.

The ricercar originally evolved out of lute music, to become a popular contrapuntal instrumental form. Its texture is fugue-like, or at any rate imitative. Thus Praetorius writes:[84] 'The *ricercare* demands diligent search and study: the handling of a good fugue must be done with special diligence and concerted thought.' A notable feature of the ricercar is that it does not keep to a single theme but consists of several overlapping sections. In this respect it resembles the structure of the motet. The fantasia, on the other hand, has a clear tendency towards thematic unity and is formally closer to the canzona.[85]

Many sixteenth- and seventeenth-century ricercars, canzonas and fantasias that were actually composed for the organ were printed in scored versions. As various authors expressly mention, this indicates that it is quite in

Gavotte for four recorders, from Mersenne, *Harmonie universelle*, 1636

order for them to be performed by string or wind instruments.[86] Conversely, polyphonic music for instrumental ensemble may be adapted as keyboard music, by intabulation if desired.

Highlights of instrumental dance music in this period include the five-part suites by Johann Hermann Schein and Samuel Scheidt. These works, too, and the numerous dance suites written by many other composers, were performed in polychoral style for preference,[87] though mixed instrumental settings certainly continued to exist in parallel with them. The latter type of setting, according to Praetorius, was typically English:[88] '[...] a number of people, with all kinds of instruments – such as clavicymbal or large spinet, large lyra, double harp, lute, theorbo, pandora, penocorn, cittern, viol de gamba, a small treble violin, a transverse flute or recorder, sometimes also a quiet trombone or rackett – [who] make soft, sweet and delightful music in company, coming together in pleasant symphony [...]'

From the adoption of a vocal part by an instrument, or the free improvisation of an additional contrapuntal part, the practice evolved of writing 'obbligato parts to the sung music' designed for specific instruments. Heinrich Schütz, who adopted and extended the Italian style, provides examples in his *Christmas Oratorio*. In this work, particular instruments are allotted to particular characters: the recorders to the shepherds, the trombones to the scribes, the clarinos to Herod, and so on. In addition, in the choral movements (*Sinfonia, Intermedium I, Beschluss*) the instruments may be used to add tone colour to the choir, either accompanying the upper voices *colla parte* or, in the case of the

### I.

### Von denen Inſtrumentis Pnevmaticis, die vom Wind getrieben oder geblaſen werden.

**§. 1.**

Unter ſolchen Inſtrumenten mögen wohl alhier die modeſten Flöthen billig den Anfang machen/ und hat man vornehmlich derſelben dreyerley Sorten ; die 1. wird Diſcant-Flöthe genennet/ und hat zu ihrem tiefſten Ton den Clavem f. wie Nro. 1. zu erſehen; die 2. wird Alt- oder Tenor-Flöthe genennet, iſt eine gantze Quart tiefer als vorige/ und hat zu ihrem tiefſten Ton den Clavem c wie Nro. 2. verzeichnet.    Die 3. wird Baſs-Flöthe genennet/ und hat zu ihrem tiefſten Ton den Clavem f. wann nemlich in dieſen drey beſagten Flöthen alle Löcher bedeckt werden.

**§. 2.**

Flûte à bec, oder Flûte doce, pl. Flûtes douces (gall.) eine Flöthe / deren erſter Zunahme vom Mundſtück (weil es wie ein Schnabel ausſiehet) und der andere von der ſtillen Annehmlichkeit; beyder Vornahmen aber mögen entweder vom teutſchen Fleut/ Flaut/ Flöthe/ oder vom lateiniſchen Wort flare, blaſen/ derivirt werden.

**D 3**                                                                                   *Appli-*

From J. F. B. C. Majer, *Museum musicum*, 1732

recorders, doubling all the parts. In his *Symphonia sacra 'Jubilate'*[89] Schütz calls for *'duoi Flautini o Violini'* as obbligato instruments: these are descant recorders. In 1634 the recorder virtuoso John Price accompanied Schütz to Denmark. Price, whom Walther[90] describes as 'an English flautist to whom Mersennus's *lib. 2. de Instrum. Harmonie, propos. 2* refers', was a member of the Dresden Hofkapelle and directed the *lille Kammermusik* in Copenhagen. He was an outstanding performer on the schwegel, which, according to Mersenne, he could take through three full octaves, using special techniques. Capricornus (1628–1665) prescribes five obbligato recorders to accompany his bass aria 'Ich bin schwarz'. Henry Purcell generally uses recorders in pairs in anthems, odes and songs.

The recorder also has rich opportunities in opera. It was used in Italy by Monteverdi (*Orfeo*, 1603), Peri (*Euridice*, 1600) and Caccini (*Euridice*, 1600), and in Germany by Staden (*Seelewig*, 1644), Schürmann (*Der erfreuten Ocker-Schäfer angestelltes Fest*, 1691) and Keiser (*Octavio*, 1705 and *Tomyris*, 1717). Recorders were also used in the English theatre, either for music on stage or for interludes. In Marston's *Sophonisba* (1606) organ and recorders accompany a solo voice. Samuel Pepys[91] reports in his diary on a performance of Massinger's *Virgin Martyr* in which the appearance of angels is accompanied by recorder music. The 'still music of recorders'[92] is regularly enlisted to portray divine beings, miracles and celestial joy. And recorders feature in serenades, as we learn from Weigel:[93]

> *Des Klanges süßigkeit zeigt schon der Flötennahme.*
> *Die dienet zur Courtoisie bey Sternen voller Nacht.*
> *Sie ist's die offt bewegt, manch angenehme Dame*
> *wann ihre ein Ständgen wird bei stiller ruh gebracht*
> *das sie des Sanfften Betts, Sich oft wohl gar entziehet*
> *und zu dem Süßen thon, hin an das Fenster fliehet.*

(The flute's very name sounds sweet: it is the handmaid of courtesy beneath the night-time stars. It is the flute that causes many a fair lady, when she hears a serenade in the quiet air, to leave her soft bed and fly to the sweet sound at her window)

There is a wealth of material for the early baroque recorder, especially the descant instruments, in two large Dutch collections, *Der Fluyten Lust-Hof* (1646)[94] and *'t Uitnement Kabinett* (1646/1649).[95] These pieces are varied both musically and technically. Like the London collection *The Division Flute* (1706),[96] they contain fine examples of variations, an exceedingly important form of the period.

## b) High baroque

During the high baroque period, the instrument in f′ gradually became established as the principal solo recorder. Although Weigel still refers in 1740 to the 'basson flûte' as the 'foundation of the flutes', the other sizes yielded pride of place to the most versatile and tonally attractive member of the recorder family. Large numbers of chamber works for treble recorder were written, particularly in England and Germany, the chief homes of the recorder. Divisions and music written expressly for dancing, which were more typically the province of the descant recorder, gave way to works in suite or sonata form for one or more treble recorders, with or without other melodic instruments, and thorough-bass. It remained customary, however, for melodic instruments to be substituted for one another. Johann Fischer, for example, gives the following specification in a publication of 1699:[97] 'Musical *divertissement*, containing some overtures and suites in 2 parts, to be played on violins, oboes or recorders [*Fleutes douces*]'. In England, sonatas by William Corbett, Gottfried Finger, Andrew Parcham and Daniel Purcell and by foreign composers living in England such as John Loeillet (of London), Charles Dieupart, Francesco Barsanti, Giovanni Batista Bononcini and Johann Christoph Pepusch[98] were very popular. Jacques Paisible, who also worked in England, was not only a popular composer but was one of the great recorder virtuosos of his day. Walther,[99] among others, mentions him by name, and Uffenbach, describing a concert in London, writes:[100]

> The instrumental music was splendid: Pepusch, who directed everything and played the thorough-bass, was the most excellent of all. In particular, a player on a flute and another on a viol di gamba, together with Pepusch, made a quite delightful concert. The flautist is a Frenchman called Paisible, whose playing is unequalled. Herr Gramm, a nobleman from Lüneburg, who was of our company and is an amateur of the flute, wished to be his pupil, but he demanded three guineas for eighteen lessons, which deterred him [...]

The German composers Johann Ernst Galliard, Johann Christoph Pez, Johann Christian Schickhardt, Johann Christoph Schultze, Christoph Graupner, Johann David Heinichen, Johann Joseph Fux, Johann Joachim Quantz, Johann Adolf Scheibe and Johann Friedrich Fasch,[101] whose works are often highly ambitious, expanded the expressive range and technical scope of the instrument considerably. Italian composers writing for the recorder included Antonio Vivaldi, Benedetto Marcello, Francesco Veracini, Alessandro Scarlatti, Francesco Mancini and Giovanni Battista Sammartini. In Holland there were works by Servaas van Koninck, and in Belgium by Joseph Hector Fiocco and Jean Baptiste Loeillet (de Gant).[102] Works by Corelli[103] and Albinoni were published in arrangements for recorder, especially in England. In France the

Frontispiece to *Directions for Playing on the Flute*, from *The Modern Music Master*, c.1731

preference for the transverse flute was reflected in the relatively small number of works written expressly for recorder, though we nevertheless find the names Anne Danican-Philidor, Joseph Bodin de Boismortier, Michel Corette, E.Ph. Chédeville l'aîné, Jean Jacques Naudot, Jacques Hotteterre le Romain, Marin Marais, Bertin Quentin and Philbert de la Vigne.[104] Naturally, the recorder was also used in *musique champêtre* – gallant, flirtatious music which was turned out by all manner of composers and which left the choice of instruments quite open. In Lully's opera orchestra the players of the *'flûte'* also had to play the *flûte à bec*, and in many chamber works the recorder is mentioned as one among several possible instruments. Hotteterre (like Telemann in Germany) says explicitly that music for transverse flute can also be performed on the recorder; if the music lies too low for the recorder, it must be transposed (a minor third upwards).[105]

High-baroque chamber combinations involving the recorder include the following:

    i)  1–4 recorders with and without basso continuo (b.c.)

    ii)  Recorder with strings and b.c.:
        Recorder, violin and b.c.
        Recorder, viola da gamba and b.c.
        Recorder, 2 violins and b.c.
        Recorder, violin, viola and b.c.

    iii)  Recorder with wind and b.c.:
        Recorder, 1 or 2 transverse flutes and b.c.
        Recorder, oboe and b.c.
        Recorder, bassoon and b.c.

    iv)  Recorder with wind, strings and b.c.:
        Recorder, oboe, violin and b.c.
        Recorder, oboe, viola da gamba and b.c.

    v)  Recorder with obbligato harpsichord

The recorder is also combined with voice in works by Thomas Arne, William Croft, Philipp Heinrich Erlebach, Alessandro Scarlatti and Johann Christoph Pepusch,[106] among others. There are numerous as yet unpublished works by various composers for the popular combination of soprano, recorder and basso continuo.

Many solo concertos testify to the recorder's high status as a concertante instrument. Besides the works of Bach and Telemann, there are concertos by

Antonio Vivaldi, Alessandro Scarlatti, Christoph Graupner, Johann Christoph Schultze (for one recorder), Johann Christoph Pez (for two recorders), Johann David Heinichen (for four recorders) and Johann Georg Graun (for recorder and violin).[107] In England, in addition to the 'concert flute' (or 'common flute'), the use of 'third', 'fifth', 'sixth' and 'octave' flutes was customary. These names indicate the interval separating the pitch of the instrument in question from the pitch of the f′ recorder. Concertos for sixth-flute were written by Robert Woodcock, William Babell and John Baston, well known in his own time as a recorder player. Guiseppe Sammartini's highly rewarding concerto, rightly often played today, is written for the fifth-flute, i.e. a descant recorder in c″.[108]

Johann Sebastian Bach enriched the recorder repertoire immeasurably. Many of his sacred and secular cantatas contain glorious obbligato recorder parts for up to three instruments, both in arias and in *accompagnato* recitatives. The recorder (which Bach, in conformity with contemporary usage, almost always refers to as *'flauto'*) is used in cantatas BWV 13, 18, 25, 39, 46, 65, 71, 81, 106, 119, 122, 127, 142, 152, 161, 175, 180, 182, 189, 208 and 217.[109] These parts are written for the treble recorder in f′, with a compass from f′ to g‴. The fact that there are differences of compass in the early cantatas almost certainly does not mean that other types of recorder were being used, as was long assumed. The reason for these differences is the transpositions of the instrumentarium that were made necessary by differences in *Chorton*.[110] The only way of solving the problem of performing these cantatas today is either to use recorders built to special tunings (from a whole tone to a minor third lower) or to transpose the instrumentarium in its entirety. Neumann writes:[111] 'Cf. the clearest cases, Cantata 152, which is given in E minor in BGXXXII: recorder compass (d′–d‴) unplayable, oboe compass (a–a″) unplayable, bass (D sharp–c′) scarcely possible. Autograph data: recorder, oboe, viola d'amore in G minor; b.c. and gamba in C minor. Upward transposition of the continuo instruments necessary, by analogy with all other cases. Vocal parts sung in transposition.' The famous *Actus tragicus* (Cantata BWV 106) can be performed using recorders at the so-called 'old' *Kammerton* (i.e. sounding a semitone lower than modern standard pitch) but transposed from E flat major to F major. This means that they actually sound in E major (in terms of modern standard pitch), into which key the other instruments and the vocal parts also transpose. The work, in other words, is shifted a semitone upwards. Transposing the work up to F major (using standard treble recorders) would be too taxing for the vocal parts in high passages.

Facing page: A musical gathering of the baroque period (Johann Christoph Steudner)

A different solution is to use treble recorders in e' flat. This instrument is also needed in Cantata BWV 13 (*Meine Seufzer, meine Tränen*), unless it is acceptable to recast the recorder part, which goes below the range of the f' instrument. The 'voice flute' in d' also occurs in Bach. The tessitura and overall compass of the two recorder parts in Cantata BWV 161 (*Komm, du süße Todesstunde*) require the use of this attractive instrument.

In two cantatas Bach prescribes a flauto piccolo. In Cantata BWV 96 flauto piccolo and violino piccolo have parts in parallel (compass f''–f''''), the flauto piccolo serving to emphasize the cantus firmus played by the violin. Cantata BWV 103 calls for a flauto piccolo with a compass of e''–f'''' sharp, again doubling the transverse flute or solo violin at the octave. In the first of these two cantatas the part can be played by an f'' piccolo recorder; in the second, a flageolet is needed (see p. 7).

Generally, Bach's cantatas use recorders '*a due*'. The use of two instruments, which calls for outstandingly well-co-ordinated playing, is not imperative, but it may be desirable on grounds of balance, given the relatively large string sections that are common today. Bach's own instructions should be taken as a guide to instrumental numbers. For normal conditions, he specifies 2 or 3 first violins, 2 or 3 second violins, 2 each of first and second violas, 2 cellos, 1 double bass, 2 or 3 oboes, 1 or 2 bassoons, 3 trumpets, 1 timpani and 2 transverse flutes or recorders.[112] In order that the recorders can be heard properly, instruments with a strong, clear and distinctive sound should be used, and the other instruments should adapt their dynamic levels accordingly. (If baroque stringed instruments are used, problems of balance are usually solved automatically.)

In line with the practice of the period, chorale movements in Bach (chorale settings in 'cantional' style in cantatas, motets and oratorios) can also be supported by wind. Bach mentions the point on a number of occasions, albeit mainly with reference to cornetts and trombones.[113] If recorders are being employed in a cantata, they can be used to accompany the cantus firmus in the closing chorale, as Bach occasionally directs. This undoubtedly helps to provide structural clarity and gives the overall sound greater brilliance. In places where the part-writing is too low or too high for the recorder's range, it can be adjusted, again following Bach's own practice.[114] In the *St Matthew Passion* two recorders are used, together with two oboes da caccia and basso continuo, to provide a highly expressive accompaniment to the tenor recitative and chorus, 'O Schmerz'. In the *Magnificat* (first version in E flat major) two recorders provide the instrumental obbligato in the alto aria 'Esurientes'.[115]

The Brandenburg Concerto No.2 is a concerto grosso, with a solo quartet consisting of trumpet, recorder, oboe and violin. This astonishing combination always used to create problems of balance because of the high trumpet in F. The problems have been resolved now that it has been possible to reconstruct the trumpet used by Bach's trumpeter Gottfried Reiche,[116] the exact nature of which had always been a mystery. The result is a clear-sounding clarino instrument with which even a recorder can hold its own in dynamic terms.

The Brandenburg Concerto No.4 is also a concerto grosso. The solo instruments here are a pair of recorders – called 'flauti d'echo' by Bach, no doubt because of the way in which they are used – and a contrasted solo violin with a highly virtuosic part. Thurston Dart was the first scholar to suggest that the recorder parts might be taken by flageolets or piccolo recorders. 'Echo flutes' and 'small echo flutes' were indeed in use in England in the early eighteenth century, and performing the work with two flageolets in G is certainly feasible. These instruments have a more delicate, and hence perhaps more 'echo-like', sound than sopraninos, which are less satisfying here. There is a detailed discussion of these alternatives in Veilhan,[117] as well as of the possible use of the treble recorder in G. The size of the instrumental forces which Bach envisaged for the Brandenburg Concertos[118] should also be taken into account. Since the timbre, responsiveness and clarity of intonation of the two recorders are very distinctive, transverse flutes are a poor substitute. It should be noted that in a transposed version of the Concerto in F major[119] Bach assigns the solo trio to two recorders and concertante harpsichord.

George Frideric Handel's four sonatas for 'flauto'[120] contain relatively straightforward writing for the recorder in a technical sense. Unlike Bach, Handel keeps to a very comfortable compass ($f'-d'''$), and the Italian cantabile of the slow movements is well suited to the tonal scope of the instrument. The so-called Fitzwilliam Sonatas[121] (named after the Fitzwilliam Museum in Cambridge, where they were discovered) consist of transcriptions by Handel himself of movements from orchestral, organ and violin works, as well as pieces for transverse flute. A trio sonata in C minor – probably a transcription made by someone other than Handel of the extant work for transverse flute in B minor – and another in F major are for a combination of recorder and violin.[122] The cantata Nell dolce dell oblio uses the particularly attractive combination of soprano, treble recorder and basso continuo, while the cantata Tra le fiamme[123] contrasts solo soprano with an instrumental ensemble of solo viol, two recorders, oboe, bassoon, two violins and basso continuo.

Handel frequently includes the recorder in his orchestras. Flauto piccolo and two treble recorders are used as obbligato instruments in Rinaldo, flauto piccolo (twice) and two treble recorders (once) in Acis and Galatea, and two treble recorders in the Resurrection Oratorio. The slow movement of the Concerto Grosso Op.3 No.1 calls for two concertante treble recorders with oboe and violin. The flauto piccolo also appears in two movements in the *Water Music*, in a bird aria in the opera *Ricardo* and in a tambourin in the opera *Alcina*, which also contains an aria accompanied by two treble recorders.[124]

Handel evidently uses the term 'flauto piccolo' to refer to the flageolet; at any rate, the autograph score of the opera *Rinaldo* contains the indication 'flageolett', while the orchestral part is labelled 'flauto piccolo'. On the other hand, there is no stylistic objection to the use of an octave flute (piccolo recorder in f″), although some flauto piccolo parts (e.g. in the tambourin in *Alcina*) include notes below the range of this instrument. A descant recorder can be used as an expedient.

Georg Philipp Telemann notes in his '*Selbstbiographie*' of 1740[125] that in his youth, driven by 'a consuming flame', he learned a great number of instruments 'besides the clavier, violin and flute'. In his '*Lebenslauf*' of 1718[126] he says categorically that 'a close acquaintance with the instruments concerned is an essential requirement in a composition'. Telemann's compositions for recorder show that he was extremely familiar with the instrument. The technical virtuosity they require is as demanding as anything in the entire recorder repertoire. Sonatas for one or two recorders, with and without basso continuo;[127] trio sonatas and quartets for all conceivable combinations of instruments; cantatas with recorder obbligato – all of these works show the clear imprint of Telemann's unmistakable style. There are some highly unusual combinations, such as those occurring in the cantata *Du aber, Daniel, gehe hin*, where the blend of recorder, oboe, violin, two viols (partly playing pizzicato) and basso continuo produces some remarkably beautiful effects.[128] The Suite in A minor for recorder, strings and basso continuo[129] is a *pièce de résistance* for good recorder players. The Concerto in C major and the Double Concertos for transverse flute and recorder and for recorder and viola da gamba[130] are alive with musicianly delight in the instruments, while expressing deep feeling.

The recorder also figures as an orchestral instrument in Telemann's suites, operas and oratorios. It is apparent from these works that it was the practice for the flautist to switch several times between the recorder and the flute within one work. Recorders and transverse flutes are scarcely ever used simultaneously, but alternate from one movement to another. A good example of such switching occurs in the Suite in C major (*Hamburger Ebbe und Fluth*).[131] In the movements that are predominantly cantabile (e.g. 'Der verliebte Neptunus') Telemann uses the flauto traverso, whereas the quick, sparkling movements (e.g. 'Die erwachende Thetis') are for the *flûte à bec*. In 'Der

Facing page: Manuscript page from Telemann's Sonata in A minor for recorder, strings and basso continuo (Ouverture)

Ouverture. 5. a Flute Conc:r. 2ter Chor, Viole 3360/5 Telemann 7.
e Basso

zufriedene Zephyr' the flauto piccolo (f″ recorder) and flauto (f′ recorder) are combined in octaves and tenths. Although flute instruments are expressly specified in only five of the ten movements of the suite, they can certainly be used at suitable points in the other movements too, in conformity with contemporary practice.

It is clear that Telemann wrote some of his recorder works for Michael Böhm,[132] who held the post of *Kammermusikus* in Hesse-Darmstadt and is one of the few recorder virtuosos of the period known to us by name. In his '*Lebenslauf*'[133] Telemann includes him among the '*musicos* who are now regarded as the most renowned. As Mr. Pisendel excels on the violin in Dresden, so Mr. Böhm excels on the oboe, flûte traverse and flûte à bec in Darmstadt.' Telemann's *Kleine Kammermusik* (*Partiten für diverse Instrumente*)[134] was written for Böhm and two other musicians. Although these partitas were primarily intended for the oboe, some of them are very suitable for the recorder. The transcription of the D major Concerto for transverse flute into F major for the recorder by Christoph Graupner and Gottfried Grünewald[135] was probably also done for Böhm. The note a‴ which occurs a few times in Telemann (c⁗ in the F major Concerto and the F major Sonata)[136] indicates the use of narrow-bore instruments, which would have 'spoken' appreciably better in the higher rather than the lower registers.

In the first half of the eighteenth century flautists were still expected to display equal mastery on the recorder and the transverse flute. The transverse flute, however, gradually emerged as the dominant partner. Referring to the still meagre literature composed specifically for the transverse flute, Quantz says:[137] 'At that time, pieces composed expressly for the flute were still quite rare. Flautists made do as best they could, arranging pieces for oboe and violin for their own instrument.' And he adds: 'I scarcely know whether it even needs to be said that the six duets that follow, although in fact composed for two flûtes traversières, may nevertheless be performed on other instruments. For example [...] on two flûtes à bec, a minor third higher.' This suggests that it may often be possible for flute music to be performed on the recorder even when the composer has made no explicit instruction to this effect. J. S. Bach's sonatas for transverse flute[138] and the solo fantasies by Telemann[139] are particularly good cases in point. More and more composers, however, came to write works specifically for the flute, which, in the words of contemporaries, was better able to 'make affecting sighs and complaints' than the recorder. Hubert le Blanc, a defender of the virtues of the viola da gamba against the 'assaults of the violoncello',[140] evidently still retains a hankering preference for the recorder. He compares the two instruments as follows: 'The harmony of the transverse flute is masculine, since it sounds harsh when next to the ear. To be very close to the instrument is never very pleasant. From a distance, however, its tone is rounded and vigorous. By contrast, the harmony of the recorder is feminine, delicate and melodious when close to the ear, and seems to have resonance. In this it resembles the voice of Mlle Quenel [...] rather than the voice of a novice such as Patchini, which, although more rounded, is also harsher and poor in resonance.' Other writers credit the 'insinuant' tone[141] of the transverse flute with attracting its many devotees. Whatever the various reasons for the change in taste, by the middle of the eighteenth century the recorder, which 'in our present musical century' is familiar to the point of satiety',[142] had been supplanted by the transverse flute.

In some works recorder and flute are used together. This delightful combination is found in orchestral music and also in some chamber works. Telemann's Quartet in D minor[143] uses a recorder and two flutes. (Interestingly, according to Telemann the recorder part can also be played by a bassoon.) The recorder is plainly the solo instrument in this piece, being favoured with a higher register than the very low-lying *traverse*. In Fasch's Quartet in G major[144] the roles are reversed: the transverse flute has the virtuoso solo part, while the recorders are mainly restricted to accompanying figuration. In Quantz's Trio Sonata in C major[145] and Telemann's Double Concerto in E minor the two instruments are used on equal terms. The B minor Quintet by Loeillet[146] uses contrasting pairs of flutes and recorders. Loeillet prescribes two *flauti di voce*, but since the parts scarcely ever go below the compass of the standard modern f′ treble recorder, this fine work can be played on these instruments with only minimal adaptation of the notated text. From the point of view of timbre, however, 'voice flutes' are certainly preferable.

The voice flute in d′ and the tenor recorder in c′ can be used for works which were originally intended for other instruments. This practice is also referred to in the literature. The celebrated woodwind instrument maker Thomas Stanesby junior discusses the advantages of the tenor recorder in some detail (1732):[147]

> Therefore, in order to reinstate this Instrument to your favours, and also to encourage the Art and Mystery of making good and perfect Instruments, I propose to produce the Flute to an equal pitch and Compass with the Hoboy, or Transverse Flute, so that any Musick written for those Instruments, or for the Violin in their Compass, shall be play'd by the Flute in Concert a unison to them, without the trouble of Transposing or writing out parts for the Flute [...]

Stanesby does not expect his proposal to meet with immediate success, 'because many Gentlemen who have taken much pains to attain the handling of the F–Flute, may be unwilling to learn a new Scale'. Today a number of instrument manufacturers have returned to making fourth-, sixth- and voice flutes. Excellent examples of the standard tenor recorder are also now available, following a long period when the instrument was somewhat neglected and used merely for consort playing.

## Stylistic questions in the seventeenth and eighteenth centuries

### a) Articulation

The differences between the Italian and French styles which evolved in the course of the sixteenth century were discussed by many authors of the period. These differences included contrasting styles of articulation. Generally speaking, the Italian style was characterized by a flowing cantabile type of articulation, whereas the French style was noted for precision in tonguing and bowing. These styles were not, however, defined by national or regional boundaries, and in Germany both styles were found side by side. Articulation was also dependent on the instrumental forces used and on the available performance space. When the recorder was used in vocal works, a cantabile style, with predominantly smooth tonguing, was required. Heinrich Schütz[148] preferred a 'steady, sustained' method of playing, which, to his regret, was 'neither known nor practised' in Germany. Christoph Demantius (1656) deplored the articulation that results, for example, from a meaningless detached '*Cantahahahahahahate*'.[149] On the other hand, when applied appropriately, short, detached playing might also be used in music combining voices and instruments. The shepherds' 'Lasset uns nun gehen [...]' in Schütz's *Christmas Oratorio*, for example, should be imitated by the recorders: smooth, less definite tonguing would be unsuitable. The sort of lightly detached choral '*falala*' articulation commonly used in refrains could also be used by the instrumentalist in the right musical context. Literary principles of rhetoric found their echo in music: a musician's playing should be 'eloquent' and expressive, and the great cellist Vandini was praised in 1770 on the grounds that he played '*a parlare*, that is, in such a manner as to make his instrument speak'.[150]

Dance music was generally played with light, elegant articulation. Canzonas, too, which were often tailored to wind instruments (with a motivic use of note-repetition), required extremely clear attack. In general, the appropriate style of articulation and method of tonguing in a piece were determined not only by the expressive content but by the form and other structural features.

References to the use of legato in the seventeenth-century literature are fairly common. The slur is introduced as a legato sign in about 1600, although at first almost exclusively to link two notes separated by the interval of a second. Heinrich Albert,[151] André Raison[152] and, earlier, Tomas a Santa Maria[153] and Girolamo Diruta[154] refer to legato primarily in the context of keyboard playing. Legato was familiar on other instruments, however, and indeed varied types of articulation arise more naturally with strings and, especially, wind than they do with keyboard instruments. The only acknowledged way of producing keyboard articulation in this period was by using the fingers; wrist and arm technique were unknown. Praetorius[155] mentions the replacement of ligatures by slurs. Samuel Scheidt[156] refers to the 'pleasant and delightful *concentus*' produced by slurred playing. Andreas Hammerschmidt,[157] in 1642, says that in addition to the soft sliding manner of playing notes of the same pitch (♩♩♩♩), 'this slurred manner must also be remembered' (♩♩ ♩♩ ♩♩) .

An examination of original slurs shows that they are mainly used with passing notes, suspensions and other non-harmonic notes. The slur serves to make clearer the dependent nature of these dissonances by linking them to other notes. This form of legato continues to apply, in broad terms, into the eighteenth century.

If a composer stipulates an occasional legato in a piece, the slurring can often be extended to parallel passages. This should not be an inflexible rule, however, since variety may also have been a *desideratum*. Ernst Kurth[158] attaches great importance to the 'principle of contrast' in later baroque music. This principle applies not only to formal structure but to tempo, dynamics and articulation.

In the high-baroque period non-legato is still the main form of articulation. French and French-influenced music, especially, shows a preference for detached playing. According to Engramelle,[159] in eighteenth-century French music the normal ratio of '*silence*' (the non-sounding part of a note) to '*tenue*' (the sounding part) is 1:1. In other words, only half of the full value of the note is sounded, while the other half becomes a rest. Indeed, the *tactée* (a short tongued note) consists of only a quarter of its actual value if it is notated as a semiquaver, and is held for only an eighth of its value if it is notated as a quaver. In *airs gais* the player adds longer and more frequent '*silences*' than he does in *airs gracieux*. The dot, as a staccato sign, is uncommon. A drop-shaped symbol above a note usually serves as a mark of accentuation, either of a single note (♩ ♩) or of a whole note-group (♩♩♩). The accent is created by shortening the note in question, so that it is separated from  the others. The degree of shortening varies: in staccato passages it must be considerable, while in cantabile writing a short break is sufficient. According to Hotteterre, tonguing is gentle on the transverse flute, more pronounced on the *flûte à bec*, and strongest on the oboe. For a precise and clear attack, the tongue has to make a somewhat longer pause after the preceding note than is necessary with gentler articulation. Even allowing for a wide range of variation, then, it is clear that the non-legato style still predominates over smooth tonguing in the more virtuoso music that is written after about 1650.

Portato is used for playing cantabile lines. Quantz[160] suggests the syllable *di* for 'slow melodies, and also for cheerful yet pleasant and agreeable ones'. Hubert le Blanc[161] says that 'playing with raised bow' is imperative in performing French works, whereas expressive, broad bowing, in which 'the tone can be prolonged as in singing, and shaped like clay on a potter's wheel', is more appropriate to Italian sonatas. The marks ♩♩♩♩  ♩♩♩♩ and ♩♩♩♩ are used to indicate a very broad non-legato, but one in which there is still a clear beginning and end to each note: as Leopold Mozart says, [162] 'each note [is given] a little emphasis'.

Quantz's formulation is relevant here:[163] 'The nearer the note, the more softly it is tongued; the further it is, the more strongly.' Articulation, in other words, must take the size of intervals into account.

The use of pairs of differing syllables for smaller note-values remains extremely important. In contrast with early Italian articulation, however, there is now a growing preference for a reversed pattern:

| | | | | | | |
|---|---|---|---|---|---|---|
| Italian tradition | trochaic | de  re | le  re | le  re | le | |
| New French (and German) style | iambic | tu  tu | ru  tu | ru  tu | ru | |
| | and | tu  ru | tu  ru | tu | ru | |

NB French syllables are *turu*; German are *diri* and *tiri*. The suffixed syllables *re* or *ru* (in German sources, *ri* or *ra*) begin, not with a rolled *r*, but with a sound closer to a *d*, using the tip of the tongue.

The most important sources on the use of articulatory syllables in this period are the instruction books by Freillon-Poncein (1700),[164] Hotteterre

(1707) and Quantz (1752). It can be assumed that descriptions of articulations for the transverse flute also applied to other woodwind instruments, though Quantz's '*did'll*' may be an exception. In all these sources the main articulatory syllable is *tu* (or *ti*), with the *t* altering to *d* as the music requires.

According to Quantz, the syllables *tĭrĭ* 'are useful in passages of moderate speed, especially because the fastest notes must then always be played somewhat unequally'. In contrast with a number of other authors, who limit the use of inequality to diatonic melodic forms, Hotteterre also gives examples of paired articulation in rapid note-repetitions:

tu  tu  ru  tu   tu  tu  ru  tu   tu  tu  ru  tu      tu

and in rapid leaps:

tu  tu  ru    tu  ru  tu  ru  tu  ru  tu  ru      tu

If a phrase begins with a complete note-group, *tu* is articulated twice in succession:

tu   tu   ru   tu      ru

If, on the other hand, the initial note-group is incomplete, then a single *tu* is used:

tu   ru   tu      ru   tu   ru   tu

Compared with normal *inégales*, dotted rhythms must be played especially pointedly. The customary syllabic pattern follows of its own accord:

tu       tu  ru       tu       tu  ru       tu       tu  ru       tu

With mixed rhythms, the group of shorter notes begins with *tu*:

tu   tu   tu  ru    tu   tu  ru  tu   tu  ru  tu   tu  ru  tu   tu  ru      tu

In fast tempi, Freillon-Poncein combines this 'reversed' articulation with the usual syllabic pattern:

i)

tu ru tu  tu  ru____  tu ru tu ru   tu ru tu ru tu   tu ru

tu ru tu ru tu    tu ru tu ru tu ru tu ru

ii)

tu  tu ru tu    tu   tu ru tu tu   tu ru tu ru

tu  tu ru tu ru tu ru tu tu   tu ru   tu ru tu ru tu ru

This produces a kind of 'double-tonguing' familiar from the Italian tradition: at high speeds the articulatory group *túru*, with a stressed first syllable, sounds very similar to *teche* ( = *teke*). The traditional formula for double-tonguing, however, is never taught by the authors of the first half of the eighteenth century. Quantzian 'double-tonguing', on the other hand, clearly had wide currency, and numerous pedagogical texts of the second half of the eighteenth century adopt it. Quantz prescribes the 'little word *did'll*', which 'is used only in the very fastest passages'. He explains:[165]

> To pronounce the *did'll*: first say *di*; and while the tip of the tongue springs forwards against the palate, rapidly remove the middle of the tongue, on both sides, a little way downwards from the palate, so that the breath runs out on both sides between the teeth. This removal provides the impulse for the second syllable, *d'll*; which cannot, however, be pronounced on its own, without the preceding *di*. The *did'll* should now be pronounced several times in rapid succession: it is easier to hear how it should sound than it is for me to express it in writing. In its use, *did'll* is the opposite of *tiri*: whereas the accent in *tiri* falls on the second syllable, in *did'll* it falls on the first, thus always coming on the note of the downward beat, or on the so-called "strong" note.

Contrast between broad and short articulation is highly important in shaping baroque music. It is this basic contrast, and the many intermediate shadings which cannot be notated, that makes for richness and variety in performance. The contrast is found, for example, in three-note groups (triplets,

3/8 and 3/4 metres etc.): ♩♩♩. The combination of light and heavy articu-latory syllables – iambic *turu* in Hotteterre, *tiri* and *diri* in Quantz – creates an *inégalité* through the dynamic weakening of the subordinate syllable. This effect of the articulation is particularly apparent in fast tempi: 'the notes must be somewhat unequal'.[166]

This articulation further reinforces the practice of *notes inégales* found in French music, whereby one note becomes longer, while the other is shorter and has less stress. The result can be very close to a true legato, notably in *lourer*, which creates a triplet rhythm (♪♪♪♪ = ♪♪♪♪). With another type of *inégalité*, namely *pointer* or more pronounced dotting, the dotted note before the short note is usually very detached (♪♪♪♪ = ♪♪♪♪).

According to Corette (c.1735), the syllabic pair *turu* is outmoded, indeed absurd, and serves merely to confuse the learner. Corette prescribes simple tonguings, varying only in terms of length, which are still able, he claims, to produce the *inégalité* required. Quantz, on the other hand, in a letter of 1758, writes that like his French colleagues Blavet and Buffardin, he still uses both *ti* and *tiri* and *di* and *diri*.

The question of authentic recorder legato, or slurred playing, continues to exercise players today. It can certainly be assumed that legato articulation on the recorder, as on other instruments, was used 'in order to make a more agreeable sound and to avoid excessive uniformity of tongue movements'.[167] Hotteterre and Quantz use the slurs that are standard among their contempor-aries. It must not be forgotten, of course, that Quantz's account applies to the flauto traverso. It is extremely unlikely, however, that the recorder players of the period saw themselves as a group that was simply concerned to defend traditon, or that they fought shy of the articulatory practices of other wind players and ignored the new style. The most reliable evidence on the matter comes from works which contain articulatory markings made by the com-posers themselves. Two-note slurs often serve to express feelings of tenderness and devotion (e.g. the Sinfonia and Aria in J. S. Bach's Cantata BWV 18, *Gleich wie der Regen und Schnee*). Legato is also often used to create a contrast with virtuoso non-legato runs on the transverse flute (cf. Fasch's Quartet in G major). Slurring of larger intervals, which occurs with increasing frequency in the course of the eighteenth century – especially in flute and violin music, which was then modern – has great expressive significance. Bach uses it for the recorder in the tenor *accompagnato* 'O Schmerz' in the *St Matthew Passion*, where it is unaltered from an original transverse-flute version.

In pieces, or sections of pieces, which are improvisatory in character, larger groups of notes are often played legato (Hotteterre, *Préludes*;[168] Bach,

Brandenburg Concerto No.4, second movement). In general, there is a growing tendency within the late baroque for melodically linked note-groups to be slurred (Bach, 'Leget euch dem Heiland unter', in Cantata BWV 182; Telemann, Sonata in C major/*Der getreue Musicmeister*, third movement; Vivaldi, Concerto in C minor, F VII, first movement). Even very high notes may be marked legato (Bach, Brandenburg Concerto No.2, second movement), and so may large leaps in quick tempi (Telemann, Sonata in F major/*Der getreue Musicmeister*, third movement). Further divergences from standard practice include the extension of the slur to a following figure and the linking of a 'light' to a 'heavy' note instead of vice versa. Some further examples may serve to illustrate the range of issues involved in recorder legato:

Carl Philipp Emanuel Bach, Trio in F major, Wq.163, first movement [SL] (Bass recorder)

Martino Bitti, Sonata in G minor (*c.*1712), first movement [Bä HM]

Francesco Barsanti, Sonata in C major (1727), first movement [Bä HM]

Arcangelo Corelli, Sonata Op.5/5 in D major (arrangement for recorder, *c.*1700), fifth movement [Moe]

Jacques Hotteterre le Romain, from *48 Préludes* (1719) [S]

Antonio Vivaldi, Concerto in C minor, first movement [MuRa]

It is apparent that the change in style that took place during the first half of the eighteenth century was perceived, at the time, largely as an issue of articulation. There were vigorous exchanges between the proponents of the new, smooth and expressive mode of playing and the defenders of the old, clipped, accented style. Leopold Mozart,[169] for example, says that 'notes which belong together should be well joined together'. Nevertheless, as far as we can tell from the sources, the new style of playing made uncertain progress. Quantz was among the many who voiced their opposition, referring to Tartini's violin playing as 'organ-grinding' and calling for a method of bowing which, 'like tonguing on wind instruments, [will] produce lively musical enunciation'.[170]

The fact that the recorder has a limited dynamic range means that the player must enlist all available interpretative devices in order to give vitality to his performance. Of these, finely nuanced articulation is especially important. The recorder is an 'old' instrument, and the 'old' ideal of articulation upheld by Quantz broadly holds good: namely, that the function of articulation is to make plain the musical structure of a piece, as well as to provide embellishment. Directions such as *Cantabile, Affettuoso, Tendrement, Gay,* etc., and a piece's general allegiance to either the Italian or the French style, help to suggest the mode of performance that is appropriate.

The recorder player faces special problems of articulation when performing music not written specifically for the instrument: e.g. a transcription of a work for transverse flute.[171] Works which the composer has set for *violino o flauto*[172] also raise their own particular difficulties. The player has a choice. He can either use the instrument in a more traditional way, omitting violin-like slurs, for instance (cf. Bononcini, Divertimento da Camera in C minor, second movement). Alternatively, he may feel it proper to use the more modern ways of playing associated with the newly established instruments of the time. To opt for the latter course is to help promote a new recorder style. What is certain is that players in the late baroque period were themselves faced with the same need to make a conscious choice between these alternatives.

It should be remembered in all this that articulation in a given part is not merely a matter of contrast and melodic structure in that part in isolation. Just as the shape of a melodic line depends on the thorough-bass, so articulation is also a function of the harmony. It is important, for example, to see whether the bass entails a change of harmony with every note or only, say, with every second or third note, and to adjust the articulation of the solo part accordingly. For an example of articulation in a solo part taking account of the bass, consider this excerpt from Handel's Sonata in F major, second movement, bars 21–4:

Original:                no slurs marked
Slurs beneath notes:    possible articulation (non-harmonic notes slurred)
Slurs above notes:      preferable articulation (non-harmonic notes slurred on strong beats,
                        tongued on weak beats)

Naturally, at other times articulation will be governed more exclusively by melodic considerations themselves. Articulation can be used both to emphasize the melodic structure (e.g. two-note slurs at the end of a melodic line) and to bring out individual notes or important note-groups (e.g. portato, in a piece with mainly detached tonguing, to bring out cantabile passages, or emphasis of individual notes by means of a staccato ($\downarrow$). In ensemble music there are choices between uniformity of articulation and the deliberate use of contrasting articulation in different parts.

### b) Ornamentation

Dance and instrumental improvisation have always gone together. Because of the improvisatory element in dance movement, dance has also been a prime stimulus of ornamentation, and can thus serve as a starting-point for a discussion of the specific art of instrumental ornamentation. Just as accompaniment rhythms were improvised,[173] so bare frameworks of notes were converted, by improvisation, into real pieces of music. 'The musicians of this period,' Friedrich Blume writes, 'were well versed in improvisation and diminution – in short, in the art of converting a *res facta* into living, melodious music in the process of performance.'[174]

In the sixteenth century we can see how diminutions, originally improvised, are gradually captured in notation, at first mainly through the use of descant coloraturas in dance pieces. The following example remains consistent with the four-part texture, which must stay 'intact and undisturbed' (Finck):

Tilman Susato, Ronde (1543)
[ZfS 1]

The suites of the seventeenth century, with their often highly elaborate part-writing, offer relatively little scope for free ornamentation. On the other hand, in addition to the important cadential ornaments, there are a considerable number of set ornaments, based on flourishes that have become frozen into formulae. Pedagogical descriptions of these ornaments can be found in Caccini,[175] Banchieri,[176] Praetorius[177] and Herbst,[178] among others. The repeats of a galliard, for example, can be played with the following free and set ornaments:

Johann Hermann Schein, Suite IV [Moes]

There is room for a free ornament in the repeated cadential chord at the end of a dance movement, when the dancer makes his final bow to his partner. As a rule the coloratura is added to the upper part, but if the root of the chord is in a middle part, that part may be ornamented instead:

Performance instructions often stress the need for longer ornaments to be played in full, even if this means that the tempo cannot be held steady. For

Frescobaldi, ornamentation is such a vital element of his compositions that the tempo of a piece must, he says, be dictated by the passage-work and ornamentation in it and therefore be handled freely. Naturally, this principle applies more to free instrumental forms than it does to dance forms, where a continuous steady basic rhythm is important.

Praetorius certainly takes it for granted that 'a larger note [will be] resolved and broken up into many other fast and small notes',[179] but elsewhere he warns both singers and instrumentalists against ugly exaggeration. Ornamentation is particularly important as an expressive device: many composers use graphic coloraturas to back up the verbal meaning of key passages of the text. When mixed vocal and instrumental forces are used, an obbligato instrumental part can echo the treatment of these vocal passages, underlining the emotional expression 'with decoratively worked runs, passages and little slurs'.

'Voluntary' (i.e. free) ornamentation is particularly appropriate in pieces written in accordance with Italian precepts, whereas French composers begin to prescribe 'essential' (i.e. set) ornaments at a very early stage, listing them systematically in tabular form. The specifications given by the harpsichordists Chambonnières (in 1670) and d'Anglebert (in 1689) served for fifty years as the basis on which other tables, including those of German composers, were constructed. The *Principles* of Jacques Hotteterre le Romain (1707) go exhaustively into the question of '*agréments*', and this work also includes a detailed table of trills for the recorder. In addition, Hotteterre's *Premier Livre de Pièces pour la Flûte traversière, et autres Instruments* [...] contains valuable information on the placing of ornaments.[180]

In Hotteterre, and all other authors of the high baroque, the trill begins on the upper note and usually ends on a *point d'arrêt* (see (i)). Alternatively, instead of the sound being held right through, there can be a pause (see (ii)), and the anticipation of the cadential note can also be shortened (see (iii)):

i)

ii)

iii)

The upper note of the trill has an appoggiatura function, and can vary in length and emphasis. In some cases, e.g. when the trill is itself on an appoggiatura, it has to begin without a 'supporting' note. With the trill as with all the principal *Manieren*, the rules should not be adhered to slavishly, at the expense of the living character of the music.

The principal *Manieren* are simple and compound trill forms, the appoggiatura, the mordent, the slide (*Schleifer*), the turn, and later the *Anschlag* or disjunct double appoggiatura. These ornaments should be applied not only when indicated – either by a general sign (+) or by specific signs (*tr, t, ⱳ,ⱳ,∞,* etc.) – but often when they are not notated in any way. In this connection, it should be mentioned that there are modern editions of early theoretical accounts of ornamentation, and there have also been a number of studies providing a systematic overview of styles of ornamentation.[181]

Finger vibrato, or *flattement*, a techique already used in earlier periods, also comes under the heading of ornamentation (see p. 69). There are very few detailed accounts of the circumstances under which it was used. According to Hotteterre,[182] it may be used on all longer notes, including the final note of a phrase or movement. In his Suites published in 1718, Pierre Philidor indicates it with the mark ⱳ. These works, and Hotteterre's account, show that the ornament was regarded as a way of creating emphasis. It is used, for example, with dotted notes and syncopations, at melodic peaks and in hemiola rhythms. Changes of frequency and amplitude produced by finger vibrato are often combined with a crescendo or decrescendo on the ornamented note. The same applies to left-hand string vibrato, which is often cited as a model for wind players. According to Geminiani (1747), finger vibrato can be used 'on any Note whatsoever'; and he urges similar principles to be applied to the transverse flute.[183] For technical reasons, of course, a wind player cannot make as much use of *flattement* as a string player can of left-hand vibrato. This is no doubt a reason why breath vibrato gradually became the more frequently described form of vibrato.

The first eighteenth-century writer to discuss breath vibrato is Quantz.[184]

He distinguishes between a softer vibrato and a more vigorous form

. Quantz's account does not make plain whether the vibrato is produced by the chest muscles or the lips. He does, however, comment on the speed of the vibrato: it must not, he says, 'be violent, that is to say, trembling; but should be done calmly'. Johann Mattheson also discusses the topic, giving a detailed description of vibrato in singing. He concludes:[185] 'It is certainly possible to indicate where such trembling or hovering should take place; but how it actually happens, neither pen nor compasses can show; it must be taught by ear.' Later, Delusse[186] and Tromlitz[187] advocate a breath vibrato. Both of these authors were flautists and champions of the new transverse-flute style.

It is not clear how widely, and until what stage in musical history, breath vibrato was used as a standard ornamental device in recorder playing. A recorder player intent on reproducing a strictly historical style of playing will no doubt resolve this issue differently from a player whose approach is directed more towards the present. The important point to remember is that all forms of vibrato should serve to bring out distinctive or unusual features in the musical structure of a piece. Vibrato sound should therefore be the exception, not the rule.

As far as 'voluntary' (free) ornaments are concerned, numerous examples can be found in early instruction books, as well as in works with coloraturas provided by the composers themselves with the express purpose of demonstrating possible types of ornamentation. Ornamentation of repeated sections of melodies, movements or parts of movements, and *da capo* sections of arias is an essential feature of the performance of eighteenth-century music. Here again, players must be guided by the expressive content of the piece. They must listen to one another, imitate, and even, within moderation, outdo one another. As Quantz says, they should learn 'early, to sing and play neither simply nor too colourfully, but always to combine simplicity with brilliance'.[188]

### c) Tempo

The sixteenth century saw the replacement of the old *tactus*, or beat with 'normal' value, by the modern beat with differential accentuation. Descriptions of tempo, and tempo marks, appeared in about 1600, at first in the many instrumental instruction books of the period. These indications are ambiguous on a number of counts. Tempo was dependent on compositional features (melodic line, harmony, tone-colour combinations, rhythmic structure, instrumentation), the place of performance (chamber music, outdoor music, church music, opera), and on the temperament and mood of the player. National and regional differences also existed. On the other hand, there were a number of commonly occurring forms in which the tempo was broadly fixed. In particular, these included dance forms with their standardized rhythmic structures – a rich resource for the recorder player. The main dance forms are listed below. It should be borne in mind, none the less, that dance tempi could still vary quite considerably: in 1676 Thomas Mace, for example, describes the courante as 'very ayrey and lively', while Praetorius (1619) calls the same dance 'earnest and dignified'. Such instances of real or apparent contradiction are frequent, no doubt reflecting different local conventions.

References used below:

L'Affilard, Michel, *Principes très faciles pour bien apprendre la musique*, Paris, 1694/1717

Choquel, Henri-Louis, *La musique rendue sensible par la méchanique, ou nouveau système pour apprendre facilement la musique soi-même*, Paris, 1759

Quantz, Johann Joachim, *Versuch einer Anweisung die Flûte Traversière zu spielen*, Berlin, 1752

## Allemande

According to Praetorius,[189] the allemande is 'not so brisk, but somewhat more melancholy and slow'. Before 1600 it was probably quieter and slower still. Yet even after 1600 the following *tripla* requires that the dance should not be too fast, given the proportional tempo relation. Indeed, Pezel, who has the sound of cornetts and trombones in mind, says it should be 'as slow as possible'.[190]

As the first movement of the high-baroque suite, the allemande functions as an introduction and is calm and measured in character. The greater the degree of stylization and remoteness from danced performance, the more restrained the tempo should be. Sometimes a descriptive term such as *Allegro* is added to indicate, by way of exception, that the tempo is a lively one. Typical opening: 𝄴 ♩ | ♩ 𝄾 ♫ 𝄉

## Bourrée

A nimble dance involving hops and leaps, quicker than the gavotte: ♩ . According to Quantz, it should be played with 'short and light' strokes of the bow. Typical opening: 𝄵 ♩ | ♩ ♫ ♩ ♩ | 𝄉  L'Affilard: ♩ = 120; Quantz: ♩ = 160.  [♫]

## Branle

The branle takes various forms. The most important (according to Arbeau)[191] are: '*Branle double* and *branle simple* in moderate duple time (for older persons), *branle gay* in triple time (for the newly wed), *branle de Bourgogne* and *branle de Champagne* in quick duple time (for the youngest), and *branle de guerre*, which gets faster and faster.' The branle still crops up occasionally in the eighteenth-century French suite. L'Affilard: ♩ = 106 + 112.

## Courante

Generally speaking, until the time of Bach and Handel the French courante (3/2) was played at a more stately tempo than the Italian corrente (3/4). Quantz specifies a detached style of playing. Typical opening: ¾ ♩ | ♩. ♫♩ | 𝄉  or  ³⁄₂ ♩ | ♩. ♩ ♩ ♩ ♩. ♩ | ♩. L'Affilard: ♩ = 90 (3/2); Quantz: ♩ = 80 (3/4).

### Galliarde

The galliarde usually involved high leaps and was therefore danced slowly, although there are also contrary accounts. According to Arbeau,[192] it was 'once [danced] with care' but is now danced 'very turbulently'. Praetorius[193] prescribes 'straightforwardness and good disposition', and Thomas Mace[194] refers to 'a Slow, and Large Triple-Time; and (commonly) Grave, and sober'. By the eighteenth century the galliarde had virtually fallen into disuse.

### Gavotte

A steady to moderate tempo: ¢. Rameau-d'Alembert: 'Never extremely fast, nor excessively slow'. Typical opening: ¢ ♪ ♪ | ♪ ᵚ. Many early editions notate the rhythm as ¢ ♪ ♪ ♪ | ♪ ♪ ♪ | ᵚ, although what should be played is ♪ ♪ | ♪ ♪ ♪ | ♪ ᵚ (cf. Handel, Sonata in G minor, Op.1 No.2, or Loeillet, Sonata in G major, fourth movement). L'Affilard: $\downarrow$ = 120; Choquel: $\downarrow$ = 132.

### Gigue

Tempo indications for the gigue are fast without exception. *Presto* and *Allegro* are most common, while *Modérément* occurs only occasionally. L'Affilard: $\downarrow\!.$ = 100 (6/8) or 116 (3/8); Quantz: $\downarrow\!.$ = 160 (6/8). The same tempo indications generally apply to the dotted-note gigue known as the canarie.

### Minuet

Eighteenth-century instruction books repeatedly stress the difference between the danced and the played minuet. In the danced minuet there is a step on every second crochet: 3/4 ♪ ♪ ♪ | ♪ ♪ ♪. The beat in the danced minuet is therefore usually quite fast, to allow a comfortable $\downarrow$ step. As the minuet becomes less common as a dance (e.g. in ballets) and more often used in its played form (in suites, sonatas and concertos), so its tempo becomes steadier. As with all dance forms, the melodic and/or harmonic structure of the minuet may also affect the tempo. 3/8 and 6/8 minuets are usually faster than those in 3/4 or indeed 3/2. L'Affilard: $\downarrow\!.$ = 70; Quantz: $\downarrow$ = 160.

### Musette

This should be played 'very sweetly', in Quantz's words. French compositions are often headed '*gracieusement*'. The musette is either in 3/4 or 3/8; tempo is moderately fast. Quantz: $\downarrow$ = [also $\downarrow\!.$] = 80 (3/4), ♪ [also $\downarrow\!.$] = 80 (3/8).

Passepied

The passepied is lighter and faster than the minuet; usually in 3/8 time. Typified by frequent hemiola rhythms. L'Affilard: $\museighth\cdot = 88$ (3/8); Quantz: $\musquarter = 160$ (3/4).

Pavane

The pavane is a solemn introductory dance, dignified and refined in character; it was sometimes performed with cornetts and trombones. According to Praetorius, its solemnity even enabled it to be performed in church. Vierdanck[195] says that 'paduanas, gagliardes and arias should be played with a fairly slow beat, [while] balletts, courantes and sarabandes [require] a lively beat in the French manner'.

Sarabande

The main tempo indications for the sarabande are *Largo, Adagio, Lentement* and *Grave*. According to Quantz, its tempo is the same as that of the entrée, loure and courante, but it should be performed in a 'more pleasing' manner. There are *Presto* sarabandes by some seventeenth-century Italian composers, and also some written in England. Thomas Mace,[196] for example, describes it as 'more toyish', looser and lighter than the courante.

The way in which dances are combined in pairs is a survival of the old *integer valor notarum*. The *proportio sesquialtera* (three notes corresponding to two in terms of *integer valor*) was the only one of the various proportions used in mensural notation that continued to play any real role in music. Other proportions were either disguised *sesquialterae* or were used as purely notational conventions. Even if the proportions 1 : 3 or 3 : 4 were written, the *sesquialtera* proportion 2 : 3 was what was actually played. Pairs of dances with a single basic beat include the *Vortanz* and *Nachtanz*, the basse danse and tourdion, the pavane and galliarde, the basse danse and saltarello, and the allemande and tripla. In these pairings the melody of the round dance, in duple time, is carried over into the leaping dance in triple time. The basic pulse thus remains constant, the contrast consisting solely in the opposition between duple and triple time. In fact, a certain amount of ritardando at the changeover to the tripla is often inescapable and, generally, rigid adherence to the *tactus* may be musically unsatisfactory or technically impracticable. In the final analysis, the living process of music-making must take precedence over theory. In any case, it is clear that the proportional principle was not so much a theoretical matter as a means of practical guidance.

Eighteenth-century tempi, so far as we can reconstruct them, seem astonishingly fast; certainly, they are never too slow for modern taste. In particular, slow movements marked *Grave, Lento* and *Siciliano* should never be performed with 'oppressive heaviness',[197] though this is still often the case today. Even with the slowest tempi – in the French literature, *Largo* and *Gravement*, in Italian and German sources more often *Adagio* – there should be a sense of constant, albeit calm, forward movement. We can tell that *Adagio* in the Italian style is often slower than *Largo* from the existence of indications such as *Largo ma non adagio* (common in Handel, for example). These slow movements are particularly notable for their strong melodic character. In almost all sources *Andante* represents a moderate tempo – not a slow movement, in other words. An *Andante* movement typically has a continuous quaver motion in the bass. It should be played decisively, though not hastily; the metrical unit is the crotchet. The other principal tempi are *Allegro* and *Presto*, the latter almost always faster than the former. While there are various gradations between 'very fast' and 'somewhat fast' – *Allegro assai, Allegro di molto* and *Poco allegro* – *Presto* always denotes a very fast tempo. The term *Vivace* commonly indicates a speed between 'moderate' and 'fast'. Leopold Mozart, in 1756, still places *Vivace* between *Moderato* and *Allegretto*. The position of *Vivace* movements in many sonatas implies that the term denotes only a moderate speed, although it also implies 'lively expression'.

The marking *Adagio* at the end of a movement, often found in the seventeenth and eighteenth centuries, indicates a retardation of the tempo before the final note: 'otherwise it is cut off suddenly and is quite lacking in *gratia*'.[198] This is also the place for an improvisatory elaboration of the cadence, provided the composer has not notated one already. Staden,[199] for example, writes: 'the last note before the close is no longer subject to the measure, owing to the ornament.' Riepel says:[200] 'Simply add the words *Solo* and *Adagio*: a violinist will embellish it with *Manieren*.'

There is no unanimity concerning the meaning of the sign ₵ (in French sources often '2'). As Kretschmar says,[201] 'musicians used these signs [the *tactus* signs] quite indiscriminately'. Generally, ₵ implies a fairly quick tempo. According to Praetorius,[202] for example, 'C *Idest, lento: tardè*: slow. ₵ *Idest, presto, velociter*: fast.' Elsewhere[203] he explains that the symbol reduces the number of beats from four to two: '[...] and where the sign ₵ or Ɖ is placed at the beginning, the notes are halved *per duplam*, and must be measured in *alla breve* time (as it was called in the past)'. There are no all-embracing rules, however, determining the duration of the beat, which depends on the type of piece and/or on additional explanatory tempo indications (e.g. ₵ *Presto*). According to Niedt,[204] the plain *alla breve* beat is:

played slowly in the overture, somewhat faster in the entrée and gavotte, quicker again in the ballo, and fastest of all in the bourrée; the aria, however, is fairly slow. In triple time, the minuet goes at a faster pace then the sarabande, which must be solemn and slow; but the gigue, finally, is usually fairly lively and fast.

Marin Mersenne says that the upper limit on tempo is a speed of 16 notes per second. Modern studies suggest an almost identical perceptual threshold, namely 18 notes per second.[205] Fairly precise tempo indications are found in Michel St Lambert and Quantz: St Lambert proposes a basic tempo of $\quarternote = 112–120$,[206] while Quantz suggests $\quarternote = 66–76$. Disparities of this sort may be attributed to differences of taste and temperament as well as to factors such as performance space and instrumentation. Comparisons with other authors show that contrasts of tempo became increasingly marked in the course of the eighteenth century: slow movements became slower, and fast movements faster.

### d)  Rhythm

Polyphonic forms, by their nature, need to be played in relatively strict time, and the same is true of dance movements. Rhythm may be handled more liberally, however, in free forms such as the toccata, capriccio and prélude, and in other toccata-like movements (cf. Telemann, Sonata in C major from the *Essercizii musici*[207] and Pepusch, Sonata in B flat major).[208] Sets of variations (e.g. divisions in the *Fluyten Lust-Hof*[209] and in the collection *The Division Flute*)[210] may also be performed with greater freedom. Indeed, the practice of the period allows ritardandos when there is a concentration of small note-values.

Solo playing in eighteenth-century music, especially in France, was governed by the principle of *inégalité*. It is true that many French authors state that inequality in the smallest note-values in a piece is not customary in 'foreign' music: this may have applied particularly to music in a strictly Italian style. In German performance practice, however, a contrast between 'heavy' and 'light', especially in diatonic figures, was very common, no doubt owing to the influence of French taste. A creative performer, of course, will make use of agogic nuances whatever the style in which a piece is composed.

Correa de Arrauxo writes in 1629:[211] 'Triplets are most easily played equal, but Cabezon, Rodriguez and other great organists of our time used to play them in a more elegant and exquisite fashion, lengthening the first note of each group of three and taking the others somewhat shorter.' The use of *inégales* as a stylistic device, however, is most pronounced in the French style between *c.*1680 and 1750. The degree of inequality ranges from triplet dotting (2:1) to the ratio 9:7.[212] It is clear from all the sources that the degree of *inégalité* is usually quite small. This is likely to have been the case anyway, given the relatively fast tempi of the period, which have the effect of cancelling out such differences. The use of *inégales* often produces articulatory patterns such as an alternation between 'long' and 'short' (‿‿ ‿‿) or vice versa. This method of giving prominence to note-groups or to alterations in the melodic line is discussed by Quantz and others, using articulatory syllables.

Rhythms that are already dotted are commonly played with even more pronounced dotting. In the French overture[213] dotted rhythms are adapted so that all the short notes become the same:

Very pronounced dottings are also found in Italian music. They occur particularly in trochaic rhythms in compound triple time (so-called Lombardic rhythm):

Dotted rhythms should be played as triplets if the wider context is that of a triplet rhythm:

Handel, Sonata in A minor

In general, dotted rhythms should be adapted to the prevailing rhythm, although this is not the case when a contrast between two rhythmic patterns is precisely what the composer intends.

Some examples from Quantz's *Solfeggi* will show that *inégales*, played with the help of corresponding articulatory syllables, were not merely confined to the French style:

The following example, however, should also be noted:

*e) Suggestions for instrumentation*

Georg Rhaw[214]

Bicinium, 'Entlaubet ist der Walde'

i)  Descant recorder          ii)  Descant recorder + viol
    Tenor recorder                  Tenor recorder + lute

Cesare Gussago

Sonata, 'La fontana'

| | |
|---|---|
| Choir I | Recorders + lute as continuo |
| Choir II | Trombones + positive organ as continuo |
| Choir III | Viols + harpsichord as continuo |
| Bars 1–32 | Tutti. Repeat: choirs I and II |
| Bars 33–44 | Choir II |
| Bar 45 onward | Choir III added |
| Bar 57 onward | Choir II tacet |
| Bar 63 | Choir I added |
| Bar 67 | Choir II added |

Aurelio Bonelli[215]

Canzona, 'Artemisia'

| | |
|---|---|
| Choir I | Recorders |
| Choir II | Viols |
| Choir III | Lutes |

| | |
|---|---|
| Bars 1–17 | Tutti. Repeat: choirs I and II |
| Bars 17–26 | Choir II |
| Bars 27–48 (3/2 metre) | Tutti |
| Bars 49–52 | Choirs I and III |
| Bars 52–67 | Tutti |

Johann Hermann Schein[216]

Suite in D minor

| | |
|---|---|
| Choir I | Recorders |
| Choir II | Viols |
| Choir III | Lutes |
| Choir IV | Trombones |

| | |
|---|---|
| Pavane | Tutti |
| Gagliarde | Choirs I and III |
| Courante | Choir II |
| Allemande | Choirs I, II and III |
| Tripla | Tutti |

Further permutations of scoring are possible within the various movements, although it is desirable for each dance to have its own basic, distinctive sound. Solo instruments from one choir may also be accompanied by the instruments of another choir: e.g. tenor recorder (top part) and viols (remaining parts).

Girolamo Frescobaldi[217]

Canzona II, 'La bianchina'

| | |
|---|---|
| Canto I | Descant recorder |
| Canto II | Descant recorder |

Basso continuo: harpsichord or spinet + viola da gamba

Canzona VI, 'La lamberta'

| | |
|---|---|
| Canto I | Tenor recorder (treble is also possible) |
| Canto II | Viol or violin |

Bass: viola da gamba
Basso continuo: harpsichord + lute

## The recorder in the twentieth century

The modern period has seen a great resurgence of interest in the recorder. There were a number of important milestones in the first half of the twentieth century. In 1919 Arnold Dolmetsch built the first new recorder, and in 1926 the first modern performance by a recorder quartet took place (in Haslemere, England). The first modern recorder teaching manual was published in 1928, by Waldemar Woehl. In 1937 the Society of Recorder Players was founded in England, and 1938 saw the publication of Gustav Scheck's treatise on the recorder, *Der Weg zu den Holzblasinstrumenten.*

In Germany the recorder first spread among *Wandervogel* groups and the youth movement, and was soon taken up by informal amateur groups as an instrument for domestic music-making. The extensive literature of the past was gradually rediscovered and many new editions were published. Typical of the sentiment during these early days of the recorder's renaissance was an aspiration that recorder playing could help make music 'a part of daily life, in a human and moral sense'.[218] 'By virtue of its unpretentious simplicity', the instrument was 'the complete antithesis of modern musical machines.'[219] The recorder became the emblem of the idealistic, if sometimes too easily satisfied, amateur. As we can see more clearly today, the desire to return to quiet sounds and to true 'listening' found a natural echo in the return to early music.

The fact that the recorder is an easy instrument for beginners helped to boost its popularity. As Paul Hindemith wrote: 'There is no one who, after a few harmless attempts, could not produce something that sounds pleasant.' A vast amount of easy music specially written for the recorder was published, often to be played in combination with fiddles, viols and, occasionally, lutes. To quote Hindemith again, however: '[...] after the acquisition of an initial technique, which will be found sufficient for many unassuming pieces, a disproportionately steep ascent blocks the road to virtuosity.'[220] Many of the pieces written during this period were aimed at the player who was content to make music at the elementary level and had not made, and might well not want to make, the jump to a more advanced standard. This is, of course, one of the positive virtues of educational music, but pieces of this sort also help to explain why the recorder has acquired its reputation as a mere half-way house on the way to playing a 'real' instrument. Highbrow musicians cast the recorder in the same lowly role as the *Klampfe*, that inglorious descendant of the classical guitar and – an equally misunderstood instrument – of the lute. At best, the recorder met with slightly patronizing tolerance as an educational tool.

Today the desire for new forms of musical activity is very widespread. Once again there is much sympathy with the aim of carefree amateur music-making rather than the rigid conventions of the concert hall, the ideal being playing for pleasure by many rather than purely intellectual connoisseurship by a few. Looking back to the interwar period, we can also identify works that were a successful fusion of this baroque-like pleasure in practical music-making with sophisticated compositional techniques. Hindemith's Recorder Trio for the music festival in Plön (1932)[221] is one such synthesis, ambitious both technically and musically by the standards of the day.

The recorder gradually recovered its status, despite the low regard in which it had previously been held, through the efforts of a number of musicians who dedicated themselves, as players and teachers, to the cause of the 'new' but ancient instrument. As far as Germany is concerned we may mention the names, among others, of the recorder player Gustav Scheck; of Manfred Ruëtz, author of solidly researched teaching materials; and of the editor Waldemar Woehl. These musicians reconstructed details of historical performance practice and breathed new life into the demanding early recorder literature. From the early 1930s the chamber ensemble centred around Scheck and Wenzinger began performing early music with recorders on concert tours and at music festivals (though the latter were rare events at this time). These concerts were proof that live music-making and historical research could meaningfully complement one another.

In England, Arnold Dolmetsch (1858–1940) and his circle at Haslemere decisively encouraged a new interest in historical instruments. The names Carl Dolmetsch, Edgar Hunt and Walter Bergmann represent a vital development of recorder playing throughout the English-speaking world. They became important pioneers through countless concerts and workshops as well as through the publication of educational music and the rediscovery of old recorder music. Their initiative led many composers (among them Stanley Bate, Lennox Berkeley, Benjamin Britten, Arnold Cooke, Gordon Jacob, Walter Leigh, Cyril Scott and Michael Tippett) to write for the instrument. A wealth of recorder music was produced, enriching the amateur and domestic music scene as well as that of concert chamber music.

In Holland, a new style of recorder playing was initiated by Kees Otten and Joannes Collette as performers and teachers; and it received an important stimulus through the imaginative personality of Frans Brüggen. His pupils too (including Kees Boeke, Walter van Hauwe and Marion Verbruggen) have contributed to the high esteem in which the recorder is held today. This recently emerged 'Dutch' style is, of course, based primarily on historical practices. It has developed, however, a very personal, and in many respects modern, expressiveness. Many Dutch composers (including Henk Badings, Will Eisma, Louis Andriessen and Rob du Bois), as well as those from other countries, have encouraged this development, following Brüggen's initiative.

The unexpected 'early music boom' that has prevailed since the 1950s has, of course, opened up ever-wider possibilities for the recorder. The low esteem which was once the instrument's lot has long since given way, at the very least, to sceptical amazement at the breadth of its appeal and, more often than not, to enthusiastic acceptance. Indeed, as historical studies have expanded, so the recorder has commonly come to be regarded, quite one-sidedly, as an early-music instrument pure and simple.

Although the great bulk of the music written for the recorder certainly comes from the past, the puritanical and frequently misguided wish to copy early performance practice often led at first to a style of playing that was debatable on a number of counts. The quest for 'authenticity' gave rise to some absurd misconceptions and exaggerations, particularly as far as expression was concerned. (These strictures do not apply to fingering and tonguing technique, and indeed in recent years technical skill has gone on to unimagined heights.) Extreme alterations of dynamics on longer notes rightly provoked particular criticism. Excessive rises and falls in volume on the recorder are bad for intonation: as early authorities from Bismantova to Quantz had already pointed out, the recorder is particularly sensitive to changes in breath-pressure. There was often cause to invoke Mattheson's comment that many people 'soon tire of its gentle, laborious nature'.[222] A new generation of players has since moved away from this mannered style of playing. New answers to stylistic problems have been found, based on modern perspectives yet taking the instrument's historical background into account.

Recorder playing may now be studied as a main or subsidiary subject at universities and music conservatories. Many leading players are active as teachers, and new teachers are continuously being trained at all levels. Study courses catering for all levels of musical and technical ability have been held since the early days of the recorder revival in this century. At that time the most important courses in Germany were those organized by the Kassel *Arbeitskreis für Hausmusik*, which provided opportunities both for further study and for informal music-making. Today there are enormous numbers of teaching and playing courses of this kind, ranging from children's courses to internationally famous summer schools in early music. The recorder is also taught in master classes virtually the world over. The Festival van Vlaanderen in Bruges regularly holds a high-level competition for recorder players. In 1977 the recorder was given the status of a recognized instrument in the Munich ARD competition for the first time. For a number of years the *Jugend musiziert* competition in the German Federal Republic has given young players a splendid opportunity to demonstrate their prowess, and there are similar competitions in other countries.

Societies specifically devoted to recorder playing have been founded in several countries, with the Society of Recorder Players in England and the American Recorder Society leading the way. These societies publish their own magazines, which include important articles on performance practice and teaching. In West Germany the journal *TIBIA*, a 'magazine for friends of early and modern wind music', was set up in 1976 and has published a good number of articles on topics relevant to the recorder. Similar societies and publications have gradually been started in other countries around the world.

A few decades ago, music-publishing houses which included recorder music on their lists were the exception rather than the rule. Today most publishers offer recorder series covering a wide range of playing ability. Many of these publications are exemplary as regards both selection and editing. A good number of publishers have recognized that it is important to provide music which is genuinely suitable for the recorder. Arrangements of classical and romantic pieces, which do not fall into this category, are steadily disappearing from the catalogues. Modern editions of early music ought to contain source details and editorial notes as standard items. Most purchasers now also expect a preface with a thorough discussion of performance practice for the work in question. Editorial additions should be easily identifiable as such. The realisation of the thorough-bass should be in an authentic style and yet plain enough to allow the thorough-bass player to elaborate it in his own way: correct figuring is essential. Editorial suggestions on ornamentation are certainly useful and often valuable, but they should not obscure the original notation of the work. Their purpose should be to stimulate the player into working out his own ornaments. *Agréments* should not be written out in small note-values, as still sometimes happens.

A significant portion of newly published music in general is accounted for by new works, and this has also become an extensive field as far as the recorder is concerned. If we survey the literature, we can trace the different stages in the revival of the instrument. The period when the recorder was mainly played in the home and in amateur gatherings gave rise to an enormous quantity of *Spielmusik*, music often in folk or quasi-folk style, for every conceivable variety of instrumental forces. The literature for recorders without other instruments ranges from pieces for one player to ensembles of four recorders, and from easy sonatinas and sonatas to small-size concertante works. Music for recorder in combination with other instruments, including Orff ensembles, includes both purely instrumental and mixed vocal and instrumental compositions. As in earlier centuries, all members of the recorder family are often involved. Often, too – again in line with early practice – the recorders may be replaced by other instruments. This sort of *Spielmusik* is primarily intended for the amateur, a fact which to some extent limits its technical scope, although the musical results need by no means be second-rate.

From time to time *Spielmusik* has been dismissed as uninteresting and insignificant, especially during the period when the virtuoso possibilities of the recorder were being rediscovered and extended. This was often an understandable reaction provoked by a temporary surfeit of '*Variations on . . .*' and '*Spielmusiken zu . . .*' On closer examination, however, and with the passage of time, we can see that a large number of excellent works were in fact written in the 1930s and 1940s, by composers such as Henk Badings, Günter Bialas, Cesar Bresgen, Benjamin Britten, Wolfgang Fortner, Peter Racine Fricker, Harald Genzmer, Wilhelm Killmayer, Armin Knab, Konrad Lechner, Gerhard Maasz, Karl Marx, Walter Rein and Friedrich Zipp.[223] Later names would now include Peter Maxwell Davies, George Crumb, Hans Werner Henze and Kazimierz Serocki.[224] Furthermore, even at this level the compositional techniques and playing styles involved have not remained confined to the neo-baroque framework. Today there are serial and post-serial pieces which nevertheless fully meet the requirements of music for the amateur. New modes of avant-garde sound production have also been used. The groundwork for playing pieces of this kind is now being laid in new methods of music teaching, where innovative playing techniques are being developed through practical work and improvisation. New styles of graphic notation, which exploit the wide range of interpretative relationships between pictures and sounds, have played a particularly useful role in livening up traditional teaching methods.[225]

As we have seen, the dividing line between recreational and educational music on the one hand, and serious chamber and orchestral music on the other, can be very fluid. It was primarily as a solo instrument that the recorder entered the realms of avant-garde music in the 1960s. Composers who have written works involving recorder include Louis Andriessen, Rob du Bois, Helmut Bornefeld, Sylvano Bussotti, Luciano Berio, Will Eisma, Klaus Hashagen, Mako Ishii, Konrad Lechner, Werner Heider, Rolf Riehm and Makato Shinohara.[226] Recorder players who are also composers have contributed works for a variety of forces: Gerhard Braun, Hans-Martin Linde and Michael Vetter.[227] Besides solo music, the combination of recorder with piano or harpsichord has remained popular, though organ, lute and guitar have also been used as chordal instruments (for example, by Johann Nepomuk David, Mátyás Seiber and Peter Benary).[228] Combinations of old and modern instruments were common at an earlier period, on occasion yielding some unusual but, as it proved, successful sound-combinations (cf. Martinů, 5 recorders, clarinet and string trio; Seiber, recorder and string trio).[229]

Composers remaining broadly within the Hindemith tradition include Lennox Berkeley, Siegfried Borris, Johann Nepomuk David, Hans Gál, Paul Höffer and Hans-Ulrich Staeps.[230] The more recent break with historical continuity has given rise to new formal models. In place of suites, sonatas and sets of variations, typical works now include *Incontri* (by Jürg Baur), *Metamorphosen* (Konrad Lechner), *Gesti* (Luciano Berio), *Paintings* (Louis Andriessen), *Monologe* (Gerhard Braun) and *Hommage à ...* (Hans-Martin Linde).[231] Serial and post-serial techniques are now as common as works written in the style of the 'new simplicity', and much use is made of aleatory and improvisatory instruments, and translations of graphic notation into sound.

Recorder ensembles have been given new challenges by composers such as Frans Geysen, Martin Gümbel, Nicolaus A. Huber, Mauricio Kagel, Peter Schat and Kazimierz Serocki.[232] The recorder has also been used with tape recorder in works by Martin Gümbel, Erhard Karkoschka, Dieter Schönbach and others.[233] Klaus Hashagen, Dubrovay Laszlo and Michael Vetter[234] have combined the recorder with live electronics. There have been relatively few straightforward solo concertos in recent years, though Kelterborn's *Scènes fugitives*, Serocki's *Concerto alla cadenza*, Baur's *Concerto da camera* and Sehlbach's *Kammerkonzert*[235] should be mentioned.

The adoption of the recorder by the avant-garde in the 1960s brought with it a considerable enlargement of the instrument's traditional range of expression. Until then, the styles of fingering and articulation demanded by composers had still been comparable to those used in difficult high-baroque pieces. Players and composers alike now helped bring about a significant expansion of the range of possible sounds. Michael Vetter, in 1964, was the first writer to provide a systematic survey of these new forms of sound production.[236] He saw the recorder as 'a new instrument: its qualities as a "*flauto dolce*" combine and intermingle naturally with those of a "*flauto acerbo*", but at other times they stand in clear contrast with them, giving rise to clashes of tone-colour that are more extreme than those naturally available to almost any other instrument.' The very simplicity of the recorder's physical construction means that its tonal range can be enormously extended. Since it is a keyless instrument, finger vibrato, glissandos, multiple sounds produced by overblowing and underblowing (chords and harmonies) and other effects are particularly easy to produce. The natural range of three octaves and the clear contrast between dynamic regions (e.g. soft low notes, powerful high notes) have been exploited. The new musical language has also created sizeable new challenges in fingering technique. At first, these seemed extraordinary, in view of the fact that previously even chromatic writing had been used quite sparingly for the instrument. Now, however, chromatic notes and micro-intervals were introduced, systematic sets of *piano* and *forte* fingerings were devised, and, altogether, a wholly new armoury of techniques was built up in a process of constant experimentation.

This brief survey of the modern recorder repertoire shows how enormously popular the instrument has become and how varied its uses now are. There are no longer problems of determining the instrumentation of a piece, since composers now state their intentions explicitly. Questions of tempo can almost always be resolved without difficulty. On the other hand, it would certainly be desirable if there were greater precision and agreement in the area of articulatory markings. 'Recorder legato', for example, does not always and everywhere mean 'portato'. And scores without markings, or with a confusing plethora of markings, hardly guarantee that the music will be played properly.

A vital requirement for playing contemporary music is a high level of technical skill. As a recorder player, you will find that this skill is also rewarded when you return to earlier music and discover that you can perform in a more vital and considered way. Past and present, in other words, come together in fruitful harmony.

# Notes

### Chapter 1: The Recorder

1 Martin Agricola, *Musica instrumentalis deudsch*, 1528/45; *Publ. der Ges. für Musikforschung*, Leipzig, 1896; 1528 edn, p. XII

2 R. Streich, 'Physikalisch, mechanische, akustische Grundlagen von Musikinstrumenten', technical report, Siemens-Schuckert-Werke AG, Berlin, n.d., p. 18

3 Francis Bacon, *Natural History*, cent. II, § 167

4 Dietz Degen, *Zur Geschichte der Blockflöte in den germanischen Ländern*, Kassel, 1939, p. 69

5 Marin Mersenne, *Harmonie universelle*, Paris, 1636/37, *Traités des instruments*; new edn, The Hague, 1957, p. 241

6 Degen, op. cit., p. 115

7 J. J. R.[ibock], *Bemerkungen über die Flöte* [...], Stendal, 1782, p. 43

8 Johann Gottfried Walther, *Musicalisches Lexicon*, Leipzig, 1732; new edn, Bärenreiter, Kassel, 1952, p. 250

9 Hans-Peter Schmitz, 'Flöteninstrumente', article (§E), MGG

10 Francis W. Galpin, *Old English Instruments of Music: Their History and Character*, London, 1932, p. 44

11 Sebastian Virdung, *Musica getutscht und ausgezogen*, Basle, 1511; new edn, Bäreneiter, Kassel, 1930

12 Michael Praetorius, *Syntagma musicum*, Wolfenbüttel, 1614/19; new edns, Bärenreiter, Kassel, 1929 and 1958/59, II, pp. 34f.

13 Bertha Antonia Wallner, 'Ein Instrumentenverzeichnis aus dem 16. Jahrhundert', in *Festschrift für Adolf Sandberger*, 1919, pp. 275ff.

14 Bartolomeo Bismantova (1677), in *Basler Jahrbuch für historische Musikpraxis*, II, Zurich, 1978, pp. 143ff.

15 Bacon, op. cit., cent. III, §§229–30

### Chapter 2: Playing the Recorder

1 Aribert Stampa, *Atem, Sprache und Gesang*, Kassel, 1956, pp. 33ff.

2 Leo Kofler, *Die Kunst des Atmens*, 21st edn, Kassel, 1955, p. 15

3 E. Barth, *Einführung in die Physiologie, Pathologie und Hygiene der menschlichen Stimme*, Leipzig, 1911, pp. 116f.

4 Johann Mattheson, *Das Neu-Eröffnete Orchestre*, Hamburg, 1713

5 Barth, op. cit., p. 130

6 op. cit., 1528 edn, VI, p. 19

7 cf. publications by Höffer von Winterfeld, BA, and Linde, S. Similar mental aids are sometimes used in oboe teaching.

8 Hieronymus Cardanus, *De musica*, c.1546; printed in *Opera omnia*, Lyons, 1663; English translation, *Writings on Music*, Rome, 1973

9 op. cit., 1528 edn, XII; 1545 edn, p. 26

10 op. cit., II, p. 88

11 op. cit. p. 11

12 cf. Ursula Schmidt, *Notation der neuen Blockflötenmusik*, Celle, 1981, pp. 19ff.

13 Sylvestro Ganassi, *La Fontegara*, Venice, 1535; new edn, Lienau, Berlin, 1956

14 Gerbrandt van Blanckenburgh, *Onderwyzinge hoemen alle de Toonen, die meest gebruyckleyck zyn, op de Hand-Fluyt zal konnen t'een mal zuyver Blaezen, en hoe men op yedert 't*

gemackelyckst een Trammelant zal
konnen maken [...], Amsterdam, 1654

15 Jacques Hotteterre le Romain, *Principes
de la Flûte traversière* [...], *de la flûte
à bec* [...] *et du Hautbois*, Paris 1707;
new edn, Bärenreiter, Kassel, 1942

16 J. F. B. C. Majer, *Museum musicum* [...],
Nuremberg, 1732; new edn, Bärenreiter,
Kassel, 1954

17 Thomas Stanesby, *A new System of the
Flute à bec or Common English Flute*,
London, c.1732

18 op. cit., pp. 186–7

19 Michel Corette, *Méthode raisonnée*,
Paris, 1750

20 François Devienne, *Méthode de Flûte
théoretique et pratique*, Paris, c.1795

21 Jean Claude Veilhan, *La Flûte à bec
baroque*, Paris, 1980, pp. 60f.; *idem, Les
Règles de l'interprétation musicale à
l'époque baroque*, Paris, 1977

22 cf. also Gustav Scheck, *Der Weg zu den
Holzblasinstrumenten*, Potsdam, 1938,
pp. 8ff.

23 cf. Hans-Martin Linde,
*Sopranblockflötenschule für
Fortgeschrittene; idem, Die kleine Übung*,
S; Hans-Ulrich Staeps, *Das tägliche
Pensum*, UE

24 Thomas Mace, *Musick's Monument*,
London, 1676, p. 85

25 cf. 'Articulation', article, *MGG*

26 op. cit., 1528 edn, p. VII

27 Philibert Jambe de Fer, *Epitome musical
des tons, sons et accordz, es voix humaines,
fleustes d'Alleman, fleustes à neuf trous,
voiles, et violons* [...], Lyons, 1556

28 Bruce Dickey, Petra Leonards and
Edward H. Tarr, 'Die Abhandlung über
die Blasinstrumente in Bartolomeo
Bismantovas *Compendium Musicale*
[...]', in *Basler Jahrbuch f. hist.
Musikpraxis*, Zurich, 1978

29 Johann Joachim Quantz, *Versuch einer
Anweisung, die Flûte Traversière zu
spielen*, Berlin, 1752; new edn,
Bärenreiter, Kassel, 1953

30 Braun, *Schule für Sopranblockflöte*, Hä;
Linde, *Sopranblockflötenschule für
Fortgeschrittene*, S; *idem, Die Kunst des
Blockflötenspiels*, S; Braun, *Schule für

*Altblockflöte*, Hä; Höffer von Winterfeld,
*Die Altblockflöte*, Hof; Lüthi, *Die
Altblockflöte* (5 vols.), Noe; Mönkemeyer,
*Handleitung für das Spiel der Altflöte*,
Moe

31 Friedemann, *Musizierfibel*, Litolff;
Linde, *Quartettübung*, S; Staeps,
*Elemente des Zusammenspiels*, Haslinger

32 Brüggen, *5 Etudes voor vingerveiligheid*,
Broekmans & van Poppel; Höffer von
Winterfeld, *Technische Studien*, Hof;
*idem, 12 Etuden*, Hof; Linde,
*Neuzeitliche Übungsstücke*, S; *idem,
Blockflöte virtuos*, S; Mönkemeyer, *Hohe
Schule des Blockflötenspiels*, Moe; Staeps,
*Das tägliche Pensum*, UE

33 Colette, *8 melodische Studien*, XYZ;
Frederick the Great, *40 Studien*, Siko;
Höffer von Winterfeld, *Bach-Studien*,
Hof; Kölz, *Essercizi*, Dob; Waechter,
*Studien und Übungen*, Noe

*Chapter 3: Recorder Music and its
Performance*

1 cf. Hermann Alexander Moeck,
'Ursprung und Tradition der
Kernspaltflöten des europäischen
Volkstums und das Herkommen der
musikgeschichtlichen Kernspalttypen',
dissertation, Göttingen, 1951

2 Hans Joachim Moser, *Dokumente der
Musikgeschichte*, Vienna, 1954, p. 38

3 cf. *Drei einstimmige Instrumentalstücke
des Mittelalters*, ZfS 181; *Mittelalterliche
Spielmannsmusik*, BA; *Trobadours,
Trouvères und Minnesänger*, Arno Volk-
Verlag, Cologne, 1951; *Spielmannstänze
des Mittelalters*, UE (*rote Reihe*)

4 Moser, op. cit., p. 36

5 Heinrich Besseler, *Bourdon und
Fauxbourdon*, Leipzig, 1950

6 Besseler, op. cit.

7 cf. especially the volumes in the series
*Das Chorwerk* (Moes), which provide an
excellent selection of works for mixed
forces

8 Hellmuth Christian Wolff, *Die Musik
der alten Niederländer*, Leipzig, 1956,
pp. 20f.

9 Bä HM

10 Bä

11 *Das Erbe deutscher Musik*, I, 4, Bä

12 In Senfl, *Deutsche Lieder*, III, Moes, which includes music from Ott, Egenolf, Finck, Schöffer and Apiarius, Forster and Salbinger

13 Moes

14 Moes

15 cf. Isaac, *Sechs Instrumentalsätze*, Bä; *Instrumentalsätze*, ZfS; *Vier Stücke*, ZfS; *Carmina germanica et gallica*, I and II, Bä HM; *Ein altes Spielbuch* (Fridolin Sichery), S; *Carmina*, NMA; etc.

16 Bä HM

17 2 vols., S

18 *Danserye zeer lustich* [...], S and ZfS

19 op. cit., II, p. 37

20 op. cit., II, p. 68

21 cf. Degen, op. cit., pp. 119ff.

22 Degen, op. cit., p. 143

23 Christopher Welch, *Six Lectures on the Recorder* [...], London, 1911, p. 27

24 Hermann Keller, *Phrasierung und Artikulation*, Bärenreiter, Kassel, 1955, p. 32

25 cf. Keller, op. cit., p. 41

26 op. cit., p. 14

27 op. cit., pp. 187ff.

28 op. cit., p. 161

29 op. cit., p. 51

30 op. cit., vol. 3, pp. 274f.

31 Girolamo Fantini, *Modo per Omparare e sonare di tromba*, Frankfurt, 1638; facsimile edn, Nashville, 1972

32 op. cit., quoted in Dickey, op. cit., p. 152

33 Girolamo dalla Casa, *Il vero modo di diminuir*, Venice, 1584; facsimile edn, Bologna, 1970

34 Richardo Rogniono, *Passaggi per potersi essercitare nel diminuir terminatamente con ogni sorte d'instromenti* [...], Venice, 1582; in *Festschrift A. v. Hoboken*, Mainz, 1962, pp. 19–28

35 Francesco Rognoni Taegio, *Selva di varii passaggi* [...], Milan, 1620; facsimile edn, Bologna, 1970

36 Richard Erig and Veronika Gutmann, *Italienische Diminutionen; die zwischen 1553 und 1638 mehrmals bearbeiteten Sätze*, Zurich, 1979

37 Quoted in Robert Haas,

*Aufführungspraxis*, Potsdam, 1931, p. 115

38 op. cit., chapter 8, p. 14

39 Diego Ortiz, *Trattado de glosas en la musica de Violones*, Rome, 1553; Kassel, 1961, p. III

40 Scipione Cerreto, *Dell' arbore musicale* [...], Naples, 1601; in David D. Boyden, *The History of Violin Playing from its Origins to 1761*, London, 1965, p. 163ff.

41 cf. Robert Lach, *Studien zur Entwicklungsgeschichte der ornamentalen Melopöie*, Leipzig, 1913, pp. 8ff., 22ff., 389f., 393

42 cf. Hugo Riemann, *Geschichte der Musiktheorie*, Leipzig, 1920, pp. 160, 168f.; also Lach, op. cit., p. 28

43 cf. Ernst Ferand, *Die Improvisation in der Musik*, Zurich, 1938, p. 253

44 Ferand, op. cit., p. 253

45 cf. Leo Schrade, *Die handschriftliche Überlieferung der ältesten Instrumentalmusik*, Lahr, 1931, p. 15

46 Johannes Tinctoris, *Tractatus de musica*, new edns, Lille, 1875 and Regensburg, 1917; Martin Agricola, op. cit.; Diego Ortiz, *Trattado de glosas* [...], new edn, Bärenreiter, Kassel, 1961; Adrian Petit-Coclicus, *Compendium musices*, new edn, Bärenreiter, Kassel, 1954; Hermann Finck, in Paul Matzdorf, *Die 'Practica Musica' H. Fincks*, dissertation, 1957; Giovanni Luca Conforto, *Breve et facile maniere*, new edn, Hirsch, Berlin, 1922; Thomas Morley, *A Plaine and Easie Introduction to Practicall Musicke*, new edn, London and New York, 1952

47 Bruce Dickey, 'Untersuchungen zur historischen Auffassung des Vibratos auf Blasinstrumenten', in *Basler Jahrbuch f. hist. Musikpraxis*, II, Zurich, 1978, pp. 77ff.

48 op. cit., chapter 25, p. 87

49 op. cit., pp. 116ff.

50 John Banister, *The Most Pleasant Companion*, London, 1681; Humphry Salter, *The Genteel Companion*, London, 1683; Robert Carr, *The Delightful Companion*, London, 1686

51 op. cit., 1545 edn, pp. 23, 26, 204

52 op. cit., p. 116

53 Dickey, op. cit., p. 105

54  op. cit., *Syntagma*, II, p. 70

55  op. cit., *Syntagma*, III, p. 229

56  op. cit., *Syntagma*, II, p. 69

57  Sylvestro Ganassi, *Regola Rubertina*, Venice, 1542–3, translated with a commentary by W. Eggers, Kassel, 1974, p. 12

58  Costanzo Antegnati, *Arte Organica*, Brescia, 1608; new German edn, Mainz, 1958, pp. 76–8 and 84

59  op. cit., p. XXIX

60  op. cit., p. XXX

61  cf. Willi Apel, *The Notation of Polyphonic Music 900–1600*, New York, ⁴1949

62  Thurston Dart, *The Interpretation of Music*, London, 1954, p. 14

63  Georg Schünemann, *Geschichte des Dirigierens*, Leipzig, p. 54, fn. 2

64  Schünemann, op. cit., p. 64, fn. 2

65  Nicolo Vicentino, *L'Antica musica*, 1555; new edn, Bärenreiter, Kassel, 1959

66  cf. *Venezianische Musik*, S; *Musik aus dem Frühbarock*, S

67  New edn, Süddeutscher Musikverlag, Heidelberg

68  op. cit., II, p. 34

69  op. cit., II, p. 5

70  Taken from Dart, op. cit., pp. 151f.

71  Heinrich Schütz, Psalm 100, 'Jauchzet dem Herrn', BA; Johann Pachelbel, Psalm 98, 'Singet dem Herrn', BA

72  cf. Wilhelm Ehmann, *Das Bläserspiel*, Kassel, 1961, p. 47

73  Heinrich Schütz, Psalm 8, 'Herr, unser Herrscher', for four-part *coro favorito*, five-part *cappella* and basso continuo, BA; *idem*, Psalm 122, 'Ich freu mich des', for two four-part *favorito* choirs, two four-part *cappella* choirs and basso continuo, BA. See also the preface to the latter

74  ZfS 89

75  ZfS 239 (Peuerl's instructions included)

76  cf. Wilhelm Ehmann, 'Singen und Spielen. Ein Beitrag zur Kantoreipraxis', in ZfH, 1955; idem., 'Die Kantoreipraxis in unseren Posaunenchören', in *Der Chorleiter*, 1957

77  op. cit., III, p. 189

78  cf., for example, Samuel Scheidt, *15*

*Symphonien*, S Antiqua

79  See, for example, *Venezianische Canzonen* (1608), S Antiqua; Erbach, *Canzona 'La Paglia'*, Bä HM; *Italienische Meister um 1600*, Pelikan Musica instrumentalis

80  op. cit., III, p. 189

81  Giovanni Gabrieli, *Canzoni per sonar*, S Antiqua; Girolamo Frescobaldi, *Canzonen*, UE; Antonio Bertali, *Sonatella*, SL

82  Giovanni Bassano, *Ricercate, passagie ed Cadentie*, Venice, 1585; new edns, Hä and Pelikan

83  Aurelio Virgiliano, *Il Dolcimelo*, facsimile edn, Florence, 1979; new edn, LPM

84  op. cit., III, pp. 16f.

85  cf. Vincenzo Galilei, *Zwölf Ricercari*, S; Giovanni da Palestrina, *Ricercari sopra li tuoni*, S; Adam Gumpelzhaimer, *Zwölf Fantasien*, S; *Instrumentalfantasien des 16. Jahrhunderts*, Nagel

86  cf. ricercars and canzonas in *Fugenbuch*, Moes; John Bull, *3 Ricercari*, SL

87  Johann Hermann Schein, *Fünf Suiten*, Moes; Samuel Scheidt, *Suite*, NMA; Christoph Demantius, *Vier Galliarden*, ZfS; *idem*, *Newe Polnischer und Teutscher Art Täntze*, S; Melchior Franck, *Suite*, ZfS; Claude Gervaise, *Tänze*, ZfS; Haussmann, *Neue artige und liebliche Tänze*, ZfS; *Altdeutsche Tanzsätze*, NMA; Paul Peuerl, *Zwei Suiten*, ZfS; Michael Praetorius, *Sechs Tanzfolgen*, Moes; Salomon Rossi, *Sinfonien und Galliarden*, S; E. Widmann and S. Voelckel, *Tänze*, S; etc.

88  op. cit., p. 92

89  BA

90  op. cit., p. 496

91  op. cit.

92  In *The Two Noble Kinsmen*, 1634

93  Johann Christoph Weigel, *Musikalisches Theatrum* [...], Nuremburg, c.1740; new edn, Bärenreiter, Kassel, 1961

94  Fascimile edn, Amsterdam, n.d.; S (abridged); *Musiekuitgeverij*, XYZ

95  Saul B. Groen (10 vols.), Amsterdam

96  S (abridged); SL (some individual volumes)

97   Johann Fischer, *Divertissement*, S

98   Corbett, S and Pe; Finger, S, Moe and NMA; Parcham, Bä HM; Purcell, S, Boosey, OUP and UE; Loeillet (of London), Bä HM; Dieupart, Moe; Barsanti, SL; Bononcini, S and Moe; Pepusch, S, Moe and Bä HM

99   op. cit., p. 459

100  Quoted in Eberhard Preussner, *Die musikalischen Reisen des Herrn von Uffenbach*, Kassel, 1949, p. 15

101  Galliard, Ri and S (as Schickhardt, *Sechs leichte Sonaten*); Pez, NMA; Schickhardt, S, Bä, NMA; Schultze, S, Moe; Graupner, S; Heinichen, Moe; Fux, NMA; Quantz, Bä HM; Scheibe, Moe; Fasch, NMA and Moe

102  Vivaldi, S, Moe and Bä HM; Marcello, Bä HM; Veracini, Pe; Scarlatti, Bä HM and Moe; Mancini, Bä HM and Pe; Sammartini, S; van Koninck, S; Fiocco, S; Loeillet (de Gant), Bä HM, Moe, S, Noe and UE

103  Corelli, Pe and Moe

104  Hotteterre, Eulenburg and Bä HM; Danican-Philidor, Bä HM; Marais, S and Moe; Boismortier, S (*Sonaten für 3 Querflöten*); Corette, Ri; Chédeville, Bä; Naudot, Bä HM; Quentin, Bä HM; de la Vigne, Noe

105  Jacques Hotteterre, *Suite D-Dur* and *Suite e-Moll*, transverse flute and basso continuo, Ri and Ba; *idem, Sechs Suiten*, flute and basso continuo, Amadeus; Telemann, *Sechs Fantasien*, flute solo, S; J. S. Bach, *Drei Sonaten*, flute and basso continuo, Hof

106  Arne, SL; Croft, SL; Erlebach, ZfS; Scarlatti, Zi; Pepusch, UE

107  Vivaldi, S; Scarlatti, Moe; Graupner, S; Schulze, unpubl.; Pez, Vieweg; Heinichen, Moe; Graun, Moe

108  Sammartini, SL; Woodcock, SL; Babell, Zen-On; Baston, SL and Zen-On.

109  cf. Alfred Dürr, 'Zur Aufführungspraxis der vor-Leipziger Kantaten Bachs', in *Musik und Kirche*, 1950, II, pp. 54ff.

110  cf. Fred Hamel, 'Die Schwankungen des Stimmtons', in *Deutsche Musikkultur*, 1944, I/II, pp. 10ff.

111  Werner Neumann, *Handbuch der Kantaten J. S. Bachs*, Leipzig, 1953, p. 9

112  cf. Werner Neumann, *Auf den Lebenswegen Joh. Seb. Bachs*, Berlin, 1953, p. 204

113  cf. Bach, Cantata BWV 4 (*Christ lag in Todesbanden*) and Cantata BWV 64 (*Sehet, welch eine Liebe*)

114  cf. Bach, Cantata BWV 18 (*Gleich wie der Regen*) and Cantata BWV182 (*Himmelskönig, sei willkommen*)

115  New edn, SL

116  cf. Helmut Kirchmeier, *NZ für Musik*, 96

117  op. cit., p. 40

118  Neue Bach-Ausgabe, VII, 2, Kritischer Bericht

119  New edn, entitled *Konzert für Altblockflöten, Klavier und Streichorchester*, Moes

120  S, NMA, BA, Pe, Moe and Amadeus

121  Hä and SL

122  S

123  BA

124  cf. Georg Friedrich Händel, *2 Arien* for soprano, obbligato recorders, strings and basso continuo, Siko

125  See Willi Kahl, *Selbstbiographien deutscher Musiker*, Cologne, 1948, p. 200

126  Kahl, op. cit., p. 219

127  Bä HM, NMA, Pe, SL and S

128  Other cantatas with obbligato recorder are in Telemann, *Harmonischer Gottesdienst*, BA

129  Eulenburg, SL and Moe

130  Moe, Bä HM and Moe

131  BA

132  Walther, op. cit., p. 446

133  Kahl, op. cit., p. 220

134  BA

135  Bä HM

136  Bä HM, NMA and Amadeus

137  Johann Joachim Quantz, 'Lebenslauf', in Kahl, op. cit., pp. 116f.

138  Hoffmeister, Noe

139  S and Hargail

140  Hubert le Blanc, *Verteidigung der Viola da Gamba* [. . .], Amsterdam, 1740; new edn, Bärenreiter, Kassel, 1951, p. 88

141  Johann Eisel, *Musicus autodidactus* [. . .], Erfurt, 1738, p. 86

142  Eisel, op. cit., p. 56

143 Bä

144 Moe

145 Bä HM

146 Bä HM

147 op. cit.

148 cf. Vorrede, Part II of the *Symphoniae sacrae*, 1647

149 cf. Robert Haas, *Aufführungspraxis der Musik*, Berlin, 1931, p. 47; see also Quantz, op. cit., p. 326

150 Quoted in Paul Nettl, *Casanova und seine Zeit*, Esslingen, 1949, p. 32

151 cf. Vorrede, *Arien*, Part II, 1640, DDT, XII

152 André Raison, *Livre de'Orgue*, 1647; new edn, Paris/Mainz, 1898–1914

153 Tomas a Santa Maria, *Anmut und Kunst beim Clavichordspiel*, 1568; new edn, Leipzig, 1937

154 Girolamo Diruta, *Il Transilvano*, 1593; excerpts reprinted in *Vierteljahresschrift f. Mw.*, 1892

155 op. cit., III, p. 41

156 Samuel Scheidt, *Tabulatura nova*, 1624; DDT, I, Vorrede

157 Andreas Hammerschmidt, *Erster Fleiß*, 1642; *Erbe deutscher Musik*, V, 7, Vorrede

158 cf. Ernst Kurth, 'Die Jugendopern Glucks', in *Studien zur Mw.*, supplementary volume to DTÖ, I, p. 199

159 Hans-Peter Schmitz, *Die Tontechnik des Père Engramelle*, Kassel, 1953, pp. 12ff.

160 op. cit., p. 62

161 op. cit., pp. 52ff.

162 Leopold Mozart, *Versuch einer gründlichen Violinschule*, Salzburg, 1756; new edn, Frankfurt am Main, 1956, p. 42

163 Johann Joachim Quantz, *Solfeggi pour la Flûte Traversière [...]*, Amadeus

164 Jean-Pierre Freillon-Poncein, *La Véritable Manière d'Apprendre à Jouer en Perfection du Haut-Bois, de la Flûte et du Flageolet*, Paris, 1700

165 op. cit., pp. 68–9

166 Quantz, op. cit., pp. 62ff., 66ff. and 68ff.

167 op. cit., p. 21

168 Jacques Hotteterre le Romain, *L'Art de Préluder [...]*, Paris, 1719; new edn, Paris, 1966

169 op. cit., p. 108

170 op. cit., p. 312

171 Georg Philipp Telemann, *Concerto F-Dur* for recorder, strings and basso continuo, Bä HM; *idem, Concerto D-Dur* for transverse flute, strings and basso continuo, Leuckart

172 Giovanni Battista Bononcini, *6 Divertimenti da Camera*, S; Francesco Maria Veracini, *12 Sonaten*, Pe; Antonio Vivaldi, *Il pastor fido*, Bä HM

173 Thoinot Arbeau, *Orchésographie*, Langres, 1588/1596; new edn, Minkoff, Ghent, 1973

174 Friedrich Blume, *Studien zur Vorgeschichte der Orchestersuite*, Leipzig, 1925, p. 64

175 Giulio Caccini, *Nuove musiche*, 1602; new abridged edn in *I Classici della Musica italiana*, IV, Rome, 1934

176 Adriana Banchieri, *La castellina*, Venice, 1615

177 Praetorius, op. cit.

178 Albert Allerup, 'Die "Musica practica" des Joh. Andreas Herbst [...]', in *Münsterische Beiträge z. Mw.*, vol. 1, Kassel, 1931

179 cf. also Praetorius, op. cit., III, §9.

180 cf. also Hotteterre, *Suite e-Moll* for recorder and basso continuo (preface), Bä HM

181 cf. also Hans-Martin Linde, *Kleine Anleitung zum Verzieren alter Musik*, Mainz, 1958, and Hans-Peter Schmitz, *Die Kunst der Verzierung im 18. Jahrhundert*, Kassel, 1957

182 op. cit., p. 33

183 Francesco Geminiani, *Rules for Playing in the True Taste*, London, 1747; new edn, London, n.d.

184 op. cit., p. 65

185 op. cit., p. 65

186 Charles Delusse, *L'Art de la Flûte traversière*, Paris, 1756; facsimile edn, Geneva, 1973

187 Johann Georg Tromlitz, *Ausführlicher und gründlicher Unterricht die Flöte zu spielen*, Leipzig, 1791; new edn, Amsterdam, 1976

188 cf. also Quantz, op. cit., p. 332

189 op. cit., III, p. 37

190 Johann Pezel, *Deliciae musicales*, 1678;

DDT, 63

191 op. cit., pp. 111ff.

192 op. cit., p. 42

193 op. cit., III, p. 36

194 op. cit., p. 129

195 Johannes Vierdanck, *Erster Theil Never Pavanen, Gagliarden, Balletten und Correnten*, 1637

196 op. cit., p. 129

197 Hugo Riemann, *Musiklexikon*, 11th edn, Berlin, 1929, article, 'Largo'

198 Praetorius, op. cit., II, p. 138

199 Quoted in Schünemann, op. cit., p. 93

200 J. Riepel, *Grundregeln zur Tonordnung*, 1755, p. 110

201 Kretschmar, *Musica Latino-Germanica*, 1605, vol. CIII; quoted in Schünemann, op. cit., p. 74

202 Michael Praetorius, *Puericinium*, 1621, Gesamtausgabe XIX, Vorwort, p. VII

203 Michael Praetorius, *Polyhymnia Caduceatrix*, 1619, Gesamtausgabe XVII, 2, p. 403

204 Fr. E. Neidt, *Musicalische Handleitung I*, 1700, chapter IV

205 Hans-Peter Schmitz, *Singen und Spielen*, Kassel, 1958, p. 21

206 cf. Eta Harich-Schneider, *Schule des Cembalospiels*, Kassel, 1952, p. 51

207 Pe, S

208 S, V

209 S; XYZ, Amsterdam

210 *The Division Flute*, S

211 cf. Dart, op. cit., p. 141

212 Hans-Peter Schmitz, [...] *Père Engramelle*, op. cit., pp. 9ff.

213 cf. Telemann, *Triosonate C-Dur* for 2 recorders and basso continuo, Bä HM; Schultze, *Triosonate d-Moll* for 2 recorders and basso continuo, S; Pez,

*Triosonate d-Moll* for 2 recorders and basso continuo, NMA; etc.

214 ZfS, 122

215 Gussago and Bonelli in *Musica instrumentalis*, VI, Pelikan

216 Moes, IV

217 UE; LPM

218 Waldemar Woehl, *Schulwerk*, book 1, Hanover, 1935

219 Waldemar Woehl, *Blockflötenschule*, book 1, Hanover, 1931

220 Paul Hindemith, *A Composer's World*, Cambridge, Mass., 1952; paperback edn, Garden City, NY, 1961, p. 195

221 S

222 Johann Mattheson, *Das Neu-Eröffnete Orchestre*, Hamburg, 1713

223 ZfS; ZfS; ZfS, S, Bä, Moes; Boosey; S; SRP; S, ZfS; ZfS; Bä; Bä; S, ZfS; Bä; Bä; S, Bä

224 Boosey; UE; S; Moe

225 cf. Gerhard Braun, *Orientierungsmodelle für den Instrumentalunterricht/ Blockflöte*, Regensburg, 1975; Hans W. Köneke, *Skizzen zu einem neuen Blockflötenunterricht*, Celle, 1972; Michael Vetter, *Felder II. Musikalisches Projekt für Kinder*, Moe

226 SL; Moe; Hä; Ri; UE; Moe; Moe; Hä; Zen-On; Moe; Hä; Moe; Hä; Moe; S

227 Moe, Hä, Bosse; S, Hä, ZfS; Moe

228 B & H; SL; Moes

229 Bä; SL

230 SL; Bote & Bock; B & H; S; Hof; UE, Hä

231 B & H; Hä; UE; Moe; Hä; S

232 SL; Moe; Bä; UE; Donemus; Moe

233 Moe; Hä; Moe

234 Ms; Editio Musica Budapest; Moe

235 Bä; Moe; B & H; Moes

236 *Flauto dolce ed acerbo*, Celle, 1969

# Bibliography

This bibliography does not purport to be exhaustive. It contains publications of two types: (a) works which deal with the recorder in detail, and (b) works which are recommended to the recorder player even though they deal with the recorder only marginally. Recent teaching works have been included only if they contain important discussions of technique or performance practice.

Agricola, Martin, *Musica instrumentalis deudsch*, Wittenberg, 1532; new edn, Leipzig, 1896

Alker, Hugo, 'Alte und neue Blockflöten. Ein Beitrag zum Problem der Spielbarkeit, Toneigenschaften und Griffweise musealer Instrumente', ZfH, 1961

idem, *Blockflötenbibliographie. Musizierpraxis, Literatur, Spielgut*, Vienna, 1960

idem, 'Die Tenorflöte als Soloinstrument', ZfH, 1960

Arbeau, Thoinot, *Orchésographie*, Langres, 1588; facsimile edn, Geneva, 1973

American Recorder Society, *The American Recorder: a Quarterly Publication of the American Recorder Society*, 1960–

Auerbach, Cora, 'Literatur für Blockflöte', *Die Musikpflege*, 1933

Bacher, Joseph, 'Die Renaissancelaute im Zusammenspiel mit Blockflöten und Gamben', ZfH, 1939

Baines, Anthony, *Woodwind Instruments and their History*, London, ³1967

Bang Mather, Betty, *Interpretation of French Music from 1675 to 1775*, New York, 1973

Bang Mather, Betty and Lasocki, David, *Free Ornamentation in Woodwind Music 1700–1775*, New York, 1976

Barthel, Rudolf, *Aus der Arbeit eines Blockflötenchores*, Celle, 1955

idem, *Ratschläge für einen Flötenchor und seine Instrumentierung*, Celle, 1972

*Basler Jahrbuch für historische Musikpraxis*

(ed. Wulf Arlt), Zurich, 1977–

Bechtel, Helmut, 'Die Blockflöte in den veröffentlicht vorliegenden Werken G. Ph. Telemanns', ZfH, 1954

Beyschlag, Adolf, *Die Ornamentik in der Musik*, Leipzig, 1908; reprint, Wiesbaden, 1978

*Blockflötenspiegel*, vols 1–4, Celle, 1931–4

Bovicelli, Giovanni Battista, *Regole, passagi die musica* [...], Venice, 1594; facsimile edn, Kassel, 1957

Boyden, David C., *The History of Violin Playing from its Origins to 1761*, London, 1965

idem, 'Prelleur, Geminiani and Just Intonation', *Journal of the American Musicological Society*, IV, 1951

Brauer, Emil, *Blockflöte und Singstimme; Volkslied und Hausmusik*, 1935/6

Braun, Gerhard, *Orientierungsmodelle für den Instrumentalunterricht/Blockflöte*, Regensburg, 1975

idem, *Neue Klangwelt auf der Blockflöte*, Wilhelmshaven, 1978

idem, 'Gruppenimprovisation mit Blockflöten', *Bausteine*, 29, Mainz

idem,'Die Blockflöte in Musikschule und Musiklehrerausbildung', *Bausteine*, 28, Mainz

Bridge, J. C., 'The Chester Recorders', *Proceedings of the Music Association*, 1900/1

Bridge, J. Frederick, *Samuels Pepys, Lover of Music*, London 1903

Buhle, Edward, *Die musikalischen Instrumente in den Miniaturen des frühen Mittelalters*, I: *Die Blasinstrumente*, Leipzig, 1903

Cardanus, Hieronymus, *De musica, c.*1546; printed in *Opera omnia*, Lyons, 1663; English translation, *Hieronymus Cardanus: Writings on Music*, Rome, 1973 (*Musicological Studies and Documents*, 32)

Castellani, Marcello, 'The *Regola per suonare il Flauto Italiano* by Bartolomeo Bismantova (1677)', *The Galpin Society Journal*, 30, 1977

Chemin-Petit, Jeanette, 'Blockflötenunterrichtsmaterial', ZfH, 1957

Clemencic, René, 'Neue Klang- und Ausdrucksmöglichkeiten der Blockflöte', *Österreichische Musikzeitschrift*, 1971/4

Conrad, Ferdinand, 'Die Blockflöte im Klangbild der alten Musik', ZfH, 1950

idem, 'Brief an einen Blockflöten-Liebhaber', ZfH, 1953

idem, 'Die Blockflöte als künstlerisches Instrument', *Musik im Unterricht*, 1956

*The Consort*, Haslemere, Dolmetsch Foundation, 1929–

dalla Casa, Girolamo, *Il vero modo di diminuir, con tutte le sorti di stromenti* [...], Venice, 1584; facsimile edn, Bologna, 1970

Dart, Thurston, *The Interpretation of Music*, London, 1954

idem, 'Recorder "Gracings" in 1700', *The Galpin Society Journal*, 12, 1959

Degen, Dietz, 'Alte und neue Spielweise auf der Blockflöte', ZfH, 1943

idem, *Zur Geschichte der Blockflöte in den germanischen Ländern*, Kassel, 1939

idem, 'Rundfunk und Blockflöte', ZfH, 1939

de Lusse, Charles, *L'Art de la Flûte traversière*, facsimile edn, Geneva, 1973

Dittmer, Kunz, *Zur Entstehung der Kernspaltflöte*, Braunschweig, 1956

Dolmetsch, Arnold, *The Interpretation of the Music of the XVIIth and XVIIIth Centuries*, London, 1915; new edn, London, 1969

Dolmetsch, Mabel, *Personal Recollections of Arnold Dolmetsch*, London, 1958

idem, *Dances of England and France from 1450 to 1600, with their Music and Authenetic Manner of Performance*, London, 1949

Dolmetsch, Carl, 'Alte oder neue Griffweise für Blockflöte?', ZfH, 1953

Donington, Robert, *The Interpretation of Early Music*, London, 1963

idem, *A Performer's Guide to Baroque Music*, London, 1973

*Early Music*, London, 1973–

Ehmann, Wilhelm, *Das Bläserspiel*, Kassel, 1961

Enke, Ferdinand, *Spiel- und Musizierweise der Blockflöte*, Berlin, 1931

Erig, Richard and Gutmann, Veronika, *Italienische Diminutionen*, Zurich, 1979

'Erkrankungen bei Benützung von Cocopolo-Blockflöten', *Lied und Volk*, 1933

Fehr, Hans Conrad, *Über das Spiel auf der Blockflöte*, Zurich, 1952

Fisch, Samuel, 'Aus der Geschichte der Blockflöte. Ihre Geschichte bis Mitte des 18. Jahrhunderts. Die Wiedererweckung der Blockflöte anfangs des 20. Jahrhunderts', *Volkslied und Hausmusik*, 1935/6

Fitz, Oskar, 'Zweistimmigkeit oder Doppelblockflöte', ZfH, 1935

*Flauto dolce, Il*, Bolletino della società italiana del flauto dolce, Rome, 1970–

*Flûte à bec*, Bulletin de l'association française pour la flûte à bec, Paris, 1981–

Gärtner, Jochen, *Das Vibrato unter besonderer Berücksichtigung der Verhältnisse beim Flötisten*, Regensburg, 1974

Ganassi, Sylvestro, *Opera intitulata Fontegara, la quale insegna a sonore die flauto* [...], Venice, 1535; new edns, Berlin, 1956 and Bologna, 1969

idem, *Regola Rubertina*, Rome, 1542/3; new edn, Leipzig, 1924

Geminiani, Francesco, *The Art of Playing on the Violin*, London, 1757; facsimile edn, London, n.d.

Gennrich, Friedrich, 'Die Musikinstrumente der Machautzeit', *Zeitschrift für Musikwissenschaft*, IX

Gofferje, Karl, *Die Blockflöte*, Kassel, 1932

Goldschmidt, Hugo, *Die italienische Gesangsmethode des XVIII. Jahrhunderts und ihre Bedeutung für die Gegenwart*, Breslau, 1892; reprint, Leipzig, 1978

Grensser, Alfred, 'Was muss der Laie über die

Blockflöte wissen?', *Nagels Mitteilungen für Musikfreunde*, 1, 1933

Hass, Robert, *Aufführungspraxis der Musik*, vol.6 of *Handbuch der Musikwissenschaft*, Potsdam, 1931

Habermann, Günther, *Stimme und Sprache*, Stuttgart, 1978

Hahmann, Richard, 'Über den Tonumfang der englischen und deutschen Blockflötenkompositionen', *Blockflötenspiegel*, 1933

Hamel, Fred, 'Die Schwankungen des Stimmtones', *Deutsche Musikkultur*, 1944

Halbig, Hermann, *Geschichte der Klappe an Flöten und Rohrblattinstrumenten*, Heidelberg, 1924 and in AMW, vol.VI, Leipzig, 1924

Harich-Schneider, Eta, *Die Kunst des Cembalo-Spiels*, Kassel, 1939

Harlan, Peter, 'Die Blockflöte nach dem Kriege', ZfH, 1949

idem, 'Alte Musikinstrumente', *Nagels Mitteilungen für Musikfreunde*, 1931

idem, 'Die Entstehung der "Neuen Griffweise"', ZfH, 1951

idem, 'Wie kam die Blockflöte wieder in unser Leben?', *Blockflötenspiegel*, 1931

Hauwe, Walter van, *The Modern Recorder Player*, vol.1: London, 1984; vol.2: London, 1987

Heyde, Herbert, *Flöten*, Leipzig, 1978

Higbee, Dale, 'Third-Octave Fingerings in the Eighteenth Century Recorder Charts', *The Galpin Society Journal*, 15, 1962

idem, 'A Plea for the Tenor Recorder by Thomas Stanesby Jr.', *The Galpin Society Journal*, 15, 1962

idem, 'Michel Corette on the Piccolo and Speculations Regarding Vivaldi's "Flautino"', *The Galpin Society Journal*, 17, 1964

Hillemann, Willy, 'Zur Praxis des Transponierens für Blockflötenspieler', ZfH, 1937

idem, 'Die Blockflöte bei Händel', ZfH, 1939

idem, 'Die Blockflöte bei S. Virdung, M. Agricola und M. Praetorius', ZfH, 1937

Höffer v. Winterfeld, Linde and Ruëtz, Manfred, *Hohe Schule des Blockflötenspiels*, Kassel, 1956

Höffer v. Winterfeld, Linde and Kunz,

Harald, *Handbuch der Blockflötenliteratur*, Berlin, 1959

Horsley, Imogene, 'Wind Techniques in the Sixteenth and Early Seventeenth Centuries', *Brass Quarterly*, 4, 1960

Hotteterre le Romain, Jacques, *Principes de la Flûte Traversière ou la flûte d'Allemagne, de la flûte à bec ou flûte douce et du Hautbois*, Paris, 1707/1720/1722/1741; facsimile edn., Geneva, 1973; Eng. trans. of 1st edn by D. Lasocki as *Principles of the Flute, Recorder, and Oboe*, London and New York, 1968

idem, *L'Art de préluder sur la flûte traversière, sur la flûte à bec, sur le Hautbois* [...], Paris, 1719; new edn, Paris, 1966

Hunt, Edgar, 'A Short History of the Recorder and Recorder Playing in England', *Blockflötenspiegel*, 1933

idem, 'The Recorder or English Flute', *The Amateur Musician*, 1935

idem, *The Recorder and its Music*, London,1962

Husmann, Heinrich, 'Die Entwicklung des Blockflötenchores in 16. und 17. Jahrhundert und das Problem der richtigen Stimmung', *Blockflötenspiegel*, 1932

Jambe de Fer, Philibert, *Epitome musical des tons, sons et accordz, es voix humaines, fleustes d'Alleman, fleustes à neuf trous, violes, et violons* [...], Lyons, 1556; facsimile, *Annales musicologiques*, 6, 1958–63

James, Margaret, *The Piper's Guild Handbook*, London, 1926

Jöde, Fritz, 'Zur Blockflötenliteratur', *Der Kreis*, 1930

idem, *Die Volksinstrumente und die Jugend*, Trossingen, 1957

Karkoschka, Erhard, *Das Schriftbild der Neuen Musik*, Celle, 1966

Kelletat, Herbert, *Zur musikalischen Temperatur insbesondere bei Johann Sebastian Bach*, Kassel, 1960

Kinsky, Georg, 'Zur Geschichte der alten Blockflöte', *Nagels Mitteilungen für Musikfreunde*, 1931

idem, *Geschichte der Musik in Bildern*, Leipzig, 1929

Koch, Johannes, 'Alte oder neue Griffweise

der Blockflöte?', ZfH, 1952

Kölbel, Herbert, *Von der Flöte*, Cologne, 1951

Kolneder, Walter, *Georg Muffats Aufführungspraxis*, Strasbourg/Baden-Baden, 1970

Krickeberg, Dieter, 'Studien zu Stimmung und Klang der Querflöte zwischen 1500 und 1850', *Jahrbuch des Staatl. Institutes f. Musikforschung*, Berlin, 1969

Linde, Hans-Martin, *Die Kunst des Blockflötenspiels*, Mainz, 1958

idem, *Kleine Anleitung zum Verzieren alter Musik*, Mainz, 1958

idem, *Handbuch des Blockflötenspiels*, Mainz, 1962

idem, 'Artikulationsübungen für Blockflötenspieler', *Musik im Unterricht*, 1956

idem, *Sopranblockflötenschule für Fortgeschrittene*, Mainz, 1960

idem, 'Spielpraxis für Blockflötenquartett', *Jugendmusik*, 23, Mainz, 1961

Lüpke, Arndt v., 'Untersuchungen an Blockflöten', *Akustische Zeitschrift*, 1940

Majer, J. F. B. C., *Museum musicum* [. . .], Nuremberg, 1732/1741; facsimile edn, Kassel, 1954

Mang, Walter, 'Die Altflöte', *Süddeutsche Musikerzeitung*, 1931

Manifold, John, *The Amorous Flute: an Unprofessional Handbook for Recorder Players and all Amateurs of Music*, London, 1948

Marix, Jeanne, *Histoire de la musique et des musiciens de la cour de Bourgogne* [. . .], Strasbourg, 1939

Martens, Hans, 'Die Blockflöte in heutiger Zeit', *Zeitschrift für Musik*, 1931

Mattheson, Johann, *Der vollkommene Kapellmeister*, Hamburg, 1739; facsimile edn, Kassel, 1954

Mayer Brown, Howard, *Embellishing 16th-Century Music*, London, 1976

Mendel, Arthur, 'Pitch in the 16th and early 17th Centuries', *Musical Quarterly*, XXXIV, 1948

Mersenne, Marin, *Harmonie universelle*, Paris, 1636; new edn (excerpts), The Hague, 1957

Mertin, Josef, *Alte Musik/Wege zur Aufführungspraxis*, Vienna, 1978

Meylan, Raymond, *Die Flöte*, Berne, 1974

Moeck, Hermann, *Das Blockflötenbüchlein. Einführung in einen Teil des alten Musikinstrumentariums insbesondere in das Wissen um die Blockflöte, des Blasinstrumentes der Liebhaber und Kenner alter Musik*, Celle, 1941

idem, 'Ursprung und Tradition der Kernspaltflöten des europaischen Volkstums und das Herkommen der musikgeschichtlichen Kernspaltflötentypen', dissertation, Göttingen, 1951

idem, 'Die skandinavischen Kernspaltflöten in Vorzeit und Tradition der Folklore', *Tidskrift för Musikforskning*, 1954

Mozart, Leopold, *Versuch einer gründlichen Violinschule*, Augsburg, 1756; facsimile edn, Frankfurt, 1956

Munrow, David, *Instruments of the Middle Ages and Renaissance*, London, 1976

*Musical Quarterly, The*, XXXIV, 1948

*Musikantengilde*, vols.1–8, Wolfenbüttel, 1922–30

*Nachrichtendienst der Beratungsstelle für Blockflötenspiel*, vols.1–6, Wolfenbüttel, 1932–9

Neumann, Frederick, *Ornamentation in Baroque and Post-Baroque Music*, Princeton, 1978

Neumann, Werner, *Handbuch der Kantaten Johann Sebastian Bachs*, Leipzig, 1953

Nickel, Eberhard, *Der Holzblasinstrumentenbau in der freien Reichstadt Nürnberg*, Munich, 1971

Ortiz, Diego, *Trattado de glosas en la musica de Violones*, Rome, 1553; facsimile edn (3rd printing), Kassel, 1961

Peter, Hildemarie, 'Die Blockflöte und ihre Spielweise in Vergangenheit und Gegenwart', dissertation, Göttingen, 1950

idem, *Die Blockflöte und ihre Spielweise in Vergangenheit und Gegenwart*, Berlin, 1953

Praetorius, Michael, *Syntagma musicum*, Wolfenbüttel, 1614/19; facsimile edn, Kassel, 1958/9. I: *Musicae artis Analecta*, Wittenberg, 1614/15; II: *De Organographia*, Wolfenbüttel, 1619 (includes illustrations, *Theatrum Instrumentorum*); III: *Termini musici*, Wolfenbüttel, 1619

Prelleur, Peter, *The Modern Musick-Master*,

London, 1731; facsimile edn, Kassel, 1965

Preussner, Eberhard, *Die musikalischen Reisen des Herrn v. Uffenbach*, Kassel, 1949 (pp. 14, 15, 126ff.)

Quantz, Johann Joachim, *Versuch einer Anweisung die Flûte Traversière zu spielen*, Berlin, 1752; facsimile edn., Kassel, 1953; trans. and ed. by E.R. Reilly as *On Playing the Flute*, New York, 1966

idem, *Solfeggien* (with commentary by Winfried Michel and Hermine Teske), Winterthur, 1978

idem, *Capricen* (with commentary by Winfried Michel and Hermine Teske), Winterthur, 1980

Rabsch, Edgar, 'Musikinstrumente für die Volksschule', *Die Musikpflege*, 1931

*Recorder and Music Magazine*, London, 1937– . (Originally *The Recorder News*.)

Reindell, W., 'Die Verwendung der Blockflöte in den Kantaten J. S. Bachs', *Blockflötenspiegel*, 1932

Reusch, Fritz, 'Von unseren Blockflöten', *Der Kreis*, 1929

Roffmann, Lena, 'Neue Schulwerke für die Blockflöte', ZfH, 1939

Rogniono, Richardo, *Passaggi per potersi essercitare nel diminuire terminatamente con ogni sorte d'instromenti* [. . .], Venice, 1592; in *Anthony van Hoboken Festschrift zum 75. Geburtstag*, Mainz, 1962

Rognoni Taegio, Francesco, *Selva de varii passaggi secondo l'uso moderno, per cantare, & sonare con ogni sorte de stromenti* [. . .], Milan, 1620; facsimile edn, Bologna, 1970

Röhrich, Georg, 'Ein Beitrag zur Verwendbarkeit der Blockflöte', *Blockflötenspiegel*, 1932

Rolland, Romain, 'Die Musik im Leben eines englischen Dilettanten unter Karl II. [Samuel Pepys]', in *Musikalische Reise ins Land der Vergangenheit*, Frankfurt am Main, 1923

Rowland-Jones, A., *Recorder Technique*, OUP, 1959

Ruëtz, Manfred, 'Über die Artikulation beim Blockflötenspiel', ZfH, 1937

idem, 'Die Blockflöte bei Bach', ZfH, 1935

idem, 'Klang- und Spielmöglichkeiten der Blockflöte', *Musik und Volk*, 1937

idem, 'Schulblockflöten in d″ und c″. Ein kritischer Vergleich', ZfH, 1934

idem, 'Zeitgenössische Blockflötenmusik', ZfH, 1935

idem and Höffer v. Winterfeld, Linde, *Hohe Schule des Blockflötenspiels*, Kassel, 1956

idem, *Blockflötenübung* (3 parts), Kassel, 1939

Sachs, Kurt, *Handbuch der Musikinstrumentenkunde*, Leipzig, 1930; photographic reprint, Leipzig, 1977

Sargent, George, 'Eighteenth Century Tuning Directions [. . .]', *The Music Review*, XXX, 1969

idem, 'On the Pitches in Use in Bach's Times', *Musical Quarterly*, 1955

Schafhaütl, Carl Emil v., 'Theorie gedeckter cylindrischer und conischer Pfeifen und Querflöten', *Neues Jahrbuch für Physik und Chemie*, 1833

Scheck, Gustav, 'Der Weg zu den Holzblasinstrumenten', in *Hohe Schule der Musik*, vol. IV, Potsdam, 1938

idem, 'Die Flötenkompositionen G.F. Händels', ZfH, 1935

idem, *Die Flöte und ihre Musik*, Mainz, 1975

Schering, Arnold, *Aufführungspraxis alter Musik*, Leipzig, 1931

Schlenger, Kurt, 'Über Verwendung und Notation der Holzblasinstrumente in den frühen Kantaten Joh. Seb. Bachs', *Bach-Jahrbuch*, vol. 28, Leipzig, 1931

Schmidt, Ursula, *Notation der neuen Blockflötenmusik*, Celle, 1981

Schmitz, Hans-Peter, *Querflöte und Querflötenspiel in Deutschland während des Barockzeitalters*, Kassel, 1952

idem, *Prinzipien der Aufführungspraxis Alter Musik*, Berlin, 1950

idem, *Die Tontechnik des Père Engramelle*, Kassel, 1953

idem, *Die Kunst der Verzierung im 18. Jahrhundert*, Kassel, 1957

idem, *Singen und Spielen. Versuch einer allgemeinen Musizierkunde*, Kassel, 1958

Schneider, Max, 'Die Besetzung der vielstimmigen Musik des 17. und 16. Jahrhunderts', AMW, vol. 1, Leipzig, 1918

Schopf, Karl, 'Hausmusik und Volkserhaltung. Die Blockflöte bei den Sudetendeutschen', ZfH, 1936

Schreher, Paul, 'Zur Belebung des Studiums der Tenorflöte', ZfH, 1938

Schüler, K., *Die Blockflöte im Zusammenspiel*, Berlin, n.d.

Schulz, Lotte, 'Vom Flötenbau [...]', *Musik und Volk*, 1937

Schumann, Heinrich, *Die Herstellung von Bambusflöten*, Wolfenbüttel, 1939 (and *Der Kreis*, 1932/3)

idem, 'Die Herstellung von Schul- und Blockflöten aus Bambus', *Hamburger Lehrerzeitung*, 1932

Seydel, Hans Jakob, 'Über die Bedeutung der Blockflöte im Musikleben der Gegenwart', *Neue Musikzeitschrift*, 1947

*Singt und spielt*, Schweizerische Vereinigung für Volkslied und Hausmusik, Zurich, 1942–

Skowronek, Martin, 'Die Ausgleichscheibe. Eine Hilfe für Blockflötenspieler', ZfH, 1958

Stave, Joachim, 'Die Blockflöte in der Muiskerziehung der Schule', *Musikerziehung*, 1938

Steinhausen, Wilhelm, 'Zur Kenntnis der Luftschwingungen in Flöten', dissertation, Giessen, 1914

Streich, R., 'Physicalische, mechanische und akustische Grundlagen von Musikinstrumenten', Siemens-Schuckert-Werke AG, technical report, Berlin, n.d.

Tartini, Giuseppe, *Traité des Agréments de la Musique*, Paris, c.1755; facsimile edn, Celle, 1961

Thoinan, Ernst, *Les Hotteterres et les Chédevilles*, Paris, 1894

*TIBIA, Ein Magazin für Freunde alter und neuer Bläsermusik*, Celle, 1976–

Tooren, Friedrich, 'Über den Klangcharakter und die stimmliche Reinheit des Blockflötenspiels', ZfH, 1941

Tricou, G., *Documents sur la musique à Lyon au XVIme siècle*, Lyons, 1899

Twittenhof, Wilhelm, 'Klarheit tut not! Zur Stimmungsfrage der Blockflöte', *Blockflötenspiegel*, 1932

Veilhan, Jean Claude, *Les Règles de l'interprétation musicale à l'époque baroque*, Paris, 1977

idem, *La Flûte à bec baroque/The Baroque Recorder*, Paris, 1980

Vetter, Michael, 'A propos Blockflöte', *Melos*, 1968

idem, *Flauto dolce ed acerbo*, Celle, 1969

Vinquist, Mary and Zaslaw, Neal, *Performance Practice: A Bibliography*, New York, 1971

Virdung, Sebastian, *Musica getutscht und ausgezogen*, Basle, 1511; facsimile edn, Kassel, 1930

*Volkslied und Hausmusik*, Zurich, 1934–42

Waldmann, Guido, 'Die Blasinstrumente', in *Die Volkmusikinstrumente und die Jugend*, Wolfenbüttel, 1956

Walther, Johann Gottfried, *Musicalisches Lexicon*, Leipzig, 1732; facsimile edn, Kassel, 1952

Warner, Thomas E., *An Annotated Bibliography of Woodwind Instruction Books, 1600–1830*, Detroit, 1967

Weigel, Johann Christoph, *Musikalisches Theatrum, auf welchen alle zu dieser edlen Kunst gehörigen Instrumente [...] gezeiget [...] werden*, Nuremberg, c.1740; facsimile edn, Kassel, 1961

Welch, Christopher, *Six Lectures on the Recorder and other Flutes Relating to Literature*, London, 1911; abridged, *Three Lectures [...]*, new edn, London, 1960

Winter, Paul, *Der mehrchörige Stil*, Frankfurt am Main, 1964

Wit, Paul de, 'Die Entstehung der Flöte und ihre Entwicklung bis auf die Jetztzeit', *Zeitschrift für Instrumentenbau*, vol. 12, Leipzig, 1893

Woehl, Waldemar, 'Aphoristisches zu einigen Blockflötenfragen', *Nagels Mitteilungen für Musikfreunde*, 2, 1931

idem, *Die Blockflöte. Kurze Einführung in ihr Wesen, ihre Möglichkeiten und ihre Handhabung*, Kassel, 1930

idem, 'Handhabung und Verwendung der Blockflöte', *Musikantengilde*, 1928

*Zeitschrift für Hausmusik*, Kassel, 1932–
*Zeitschrift für Spielmusik*, Celle, 1932–

# Index of Names

142

# Index of Subjects

accento, accentus 71, 75, 110
'Accort' (consort) of recorders (Praetorius) 81
acoustic properties of recorder 1ff.
Actus tragicus (Bach) 92
Adagio 117
alla breve 117f.
Allegro 117
allemande 114
alta 57
Andante 117
appoggiatura 68, 75, 111f.
Ars Antiqua 53
Ars Nova 54
articulation 42ff., 63ff., 100ff.
   styles of 43ff.

balance, when holding recorder 29f.
ballade 54
ballata 55
baroque recorder 13
bass recorder 11, 58, 59ff., 61, 81
bassa 57
basset 60, 81
bassoon 60
beak, recorder 11
beginners 50, 122ff.
bell, recorder 9
bore 5, 9
bourdon 53
bourrée 114
branle 114
breath-pressure 3, 5, 22, 27
breath quantity 22, 24f.
breath support 22f.
breath vibrato 112f.
breathing 20ff.
   mouth 20
   nasal 20

snatched 21
   types of 21f.
broken consort 62

caccia 55
cantata 95f.
cantatas, Bach 92f., 105, 106
cantilena style 55
canzonetta 85
canzona 85f., 100
Capellchor (capella) 84
carmina 58
cascata 71
chamber works 89ff.
chanson 56f.
chorale settings 94
choric settings 59, 81ff.
Chorton 92
church choral music 85
cittern 62
clogging 17
colla parte 53, 54, 58
coloratura 109ff., 113
combinations of recorders (Praetorius) 59f.
common flute 7, 92
concerto, solo 91ff., 96f.
concerto grosso 94f.
conductus 53
conical bore 5, 9
contrast, principle of (baroque) 101
contrasting timbres 58
cornett 64, 78, 83f.
coro favorito 84
courante 114
court ensembles 79
crook, S-shaped 11
cross-fingerings 28
crumhorn 54, 59, 60, 78, 83f.

146